Gestalt Therapy for
Addictive and
Self-Medicating Behaviors

Philip Brownell, MDiv, PsyD, is a licensed clinical psychologist in North Carolina and Oregon and a registered psychologist in Bermuda. He is an ordained clergyman and writes a weekly column on integrative issues for *The Royal Gazette*, Bermuda's largest daily newspaper. He is currently a staff psychologist at Benedict Associates, Ltd., where he offers a broad range of assessment and counseling services to child, adolescent, and adult populations, including individual, couple, family, and group therapy. He is the editor of the *Handbook for Theory, Research, and Practice in Gestalt Therapy* (2008), author of *Gestalt Therapy: A Guide to Contemporary Practice* (2010), coeditor of *Continuity and Change: Gestalt Therapy Now* (2011), coeditor of *Gestalt!*, the official journal of the Association for the Advancement of Gestalt Therapy (AAGT), associate editor of *The Korean Journal of Gestalt Therapy*, journal of the Korean Gestalt Therapy Association, a consulting editor at the *European Journal for Qualitative Research in Psychotherapy*, and cochair of the AAGT's Research Task Force. He is a member of the New York Institute for Gestalt Therapy, the American Psychological Association, and the AAGT.

Gestalt Therapy for Addictive and Self-Medicating Behaviors

Philip Brownell, MDiv, PsyD

SPRINGER PUBLISHING COMPANY
NEW YORK

Springer Publishing Company, LLC
11 West 42nd Street
New York, NY 10036
www.springerpub.com

Acquisitions Editor: Nancy Hale
Composition: Newgen Imaging

ISBN: 978-0-8261-0695-7
E-book ISBN: 978-0-8261-0696-4

11 12 13/ 5 4 3 2 1

Cataloging-in-Publication Data is available from the Library of Congress.
Library of Congress Control Number: 2011943176

Special discounts on bulk quantities of our books are available to corporations, pro-fessional associations, pharmaceutical companies, health care organizations, and other qualifying groups.

If you are interested in a custom book, including chapters from more than one of our titles, we can provide that service as well.

For details, please contact:
Special Sales Department, Springer Publishing Company, LLC
11 West 42nd Street, 15th Floor, New York, NY 10036-8002
Phone: 877-687-7476 or 212-431-4370; Fax: 212-941-7842
Email: sales@springerpub.com

Printed in the United States of America by Gasch Printing.

This book is dedicated to
The Brownells of Lemon Street
and Mississippi Bar:
Warren, Barbara, Philip, Cathy, Mark,
Jeff and Tim–A petri dish of creativity!

Contents

Preface

Other people—Michael Clemmens and Helga Matzko come to mind—have written about a gestalt therapy approach to addictions. I am indebted to both. However, what I wanted to write was an application and extension of some of the things I had written in the preceding volume, *Gestalt Therapy: A Guide to Contemporary Practice*. I hope that this book will build on that in a way that provides therapists and counselors in substance abuse and addiction fields a guide to help them develop a way of doing gestalt therapy with their clients.

I became firmly convinced while working on a dual diagnosis (co-occurring disorders) intensive care unit when I was in my doctoral program that gestalt therapy is a very useful way to do treatment with substance-dependent clients. It is not at all the confrontational and an alarming approach popularized in the late 1960s. Although I had seen it used effectively in a unit at the Oak Knoll Naval Hospital in Oakland, California, at that time, I have since learned its theoretical base and its relational and supportive nature. Gestalt therapy, to me, has all the best of where many current psychotherapies are currently headed in their evolving convergence.

I also chose to write about this area, recovery work, because I have some personal history here. I grew up in an alcoholic home and learned what many know as a codependent way of conducting relationships. I did my own therapy around that (and other things); such is what psychotherapists are expected to do, but I also did it because I wanted to live better. So, I believe it is a worthwhile field to spend time writing about.

Many people choose to learn and practice gestalt therapy because they have been with a gestalt therapist for their personal work. I did not. I learned gestalt therapy because I had already been around it, and I realized that it made the most sense to me. So, I just felt the two of these streams came together at a point in time: my personal history and my convictions about the value of gestalt therapy.

Isn't that the way a lot of these kinds of things go?

I hope the reader will make a project out of reading this book. There are many contemporary gestalt therapists who are writing, and it is possible to work with most of them to augment this book and the previous one with personal, face-to-face training. Those from outside the world of gestalt therapy are referenced because in some way the work they have done converges with, is in consilience with, or complements the gestalt approach.

As a byproduct of the way I have written and the associations I have made to other practices, I hope the reader will also sense how relevant gestalt therapy is. In many cases, I do believe the research that has been carried out on some other approach can be said to apply to gestalt as well, and that is because the two, in some central way, share an essential and salient feature.

As I put the finishing touches on this book, I write from Southampton, Bermuda, where a tropical storm is brewing in the Atlantic, and we are finally getting some much-needed rain. The tree frogs are happy, and they are singing in a noisy chorus. In the next week, I intend to take my wife and rediscover the beach, the warm water, and the beauty of this place. Perhaps, we will watch the parrot fish splash near the surface as they chip away on the rocks. The beauty of this place is so intoxicating that one could become ... well, addicted.

Philip Brownell

Acknowledgments

Of course, I thank the people at Springer Publishing Company—Jennifer Perillo and Kathryn Corasaniti. Thank you for dealing with what I sent you.

Most of all, I thank my wife Linda. She is a people person who put "both of us doing things with people" on hold while I hung out with the computer. She hates to be stuck in the house, so she spent a lot of time doing things on her own outside and away, not wanting to bother me when I was writing. I am looking forward to us rediscovering one another. She is a wonderful person, and all my friends in the world of gestalt therapy who know her can truly get behind the phrase "his better half." She is more like my better 75%.

I also think of the people I knew along the way in my own recovery, and that brings to mind Dennis Henderson. Hi, Dennis! Thanks for all your help.

I would like to acknowledge my parents Warren and Barbara Brownell who have both passed out of this world. Thank God, truly, that I was able to reconnect with you.

Introduction

I grew up in an alcoholic home. My mother would drink beer and wine, and she would impulsively embark upon projects and adventures that required the rest of the family to accommodate her. Many times we would be off in the middle of the night after she had been drinking. Once, she was determined that we needed to drive from Sacramento to Oakland, California, through dense valley fog, to see my grandmother. We could not see much past the front fender, and we were going about 65 or 70 on the interstate. I was terrified, so I demanded to drive in order to keep us safe. I was only fifteen and a half with a learner's permit.

Another time she and one of her drinking buddies were laughing it up at the house, and she told me to kill some chickens for the barbeque. We had raised about 120 chickens, and they were all of age to be eaten. I had a friend over to spend the night, and I was mortified that my mother would be drunk in front of him, so I asked in a disgusted tone of voice, "How many do you want done?" She must have thought that I looked funny, because she and her friend looked at one another, laughed, and then she said, "All of 'em." So, my friend and I wrung the necks of all 120 chickens, and then everyone in the house spent the rest of the night plucking feathers and cleaning chicken carcasses so we could put them in the freezer.

Things were clearly out of control at times in our house. Sometimes, I could not contain myself and I would let her have some of what I really thought. I will never forget becoming upset when my parents came through the door one night; my mother was drunk, and I let her know I did not like it. She cried out that she wanted me to respect her, and I said, "How can I respect you, when you act like this?" That is when I flopped down in a chair to sulk, and my father came and stood over me, shook his head, looked disgusted, and said, "When are you ever going to learn?"

I learned. I learned to be hypervigilant. I learned to get myself out of the way. I learned to take advantage, and when I was an adolescent and wanted to fit in with my friends, I learned how to sneak my mother's horribly tasting cheap wine out of the house so we could get drunk together.

I compensated for what I learned by trying to achieve my way out of my past, and I became a professional people helper.

Does not all this sound inspiring? I am an adult child of an alcoholic, but I do not wear that as my chief identity. I spent several years in therapy and read many recovery books, including many about code-pendency, and so I know that part of life. I am familiar with the scene, and I chose not to stop there.

My mother eventually quit drinking. She went to rehab. She attended AA meetings. She also worked her way beyond mere sobriety as a goal, and eventually she moved on. Her primary identity was not that she was an alcoholic. She found a life beyond recovery, and to me that is the chief aim of recovery. If one is truly recovered, one does not simply replace one compulsion for another.

In a way, then, recovery is paradoxical. If one is successful, one finds him- or herself in another universe. There is life beyond meetings, sponsors, working the steps, and rehearsing continually one's fail-safe cards and correcting thinking errors. Relapse does not occur any longer, so one is no longer reminding oneself of the steps in the relapse cycle. One has actually recovered. One is not still *in* recovery. One has moved on and found life. Recovery is paradoxical because you achieve real recovery once you are no longer in need of it.

I know that this runs counter to the idea that addiction is a disease in which the addict has no control, and that one needs to follow the steps, keep coming back to meetings, make oneself accountable to at least one other person (like a sponsor), and constantly be vigilant to protect oneself from relapse because one is never really over this disease. I believe these things, and other kinds of things that are part of a recov-ery program, are needed at one point in the process. A person might never actually get beyond that point, and so, for such people, these are needed perpetually. However, I do not believe that one is truly recov-ered until one no longer needs "recovery." In a sense, then, you achieve it by no longer aiming at it.

This book is a gestalt therapy approach to working with people who suffer from addictive and self-medicating behaviors. It is not a paint-by-numbers approach, a cookbook with recipes to prepare a therapeutic dish or a workbook that people can fill in the blanks and learn ten ways to overcome addiction. It is a description of what a gestalt therapist might do working with clients who are addicted and want to begin in recovery (or continue beyond sobriety).

There are several parts to the book.

Part I covers the need to change. People need to change, but do they *want* to change? People need to change, but do they think they can change? What is this thing called recovery anyhow? Part one is a basic orientation to the field.

Part II covers a basic orientation the field of gestalt therapy. It is only a basic summary, but it is one that goes to the core of what contemporary gestalt therapy is all about. The reader is advised to consult the preceding volume (*Gestalt Therapy: A Guide to Contemporary Practice*) and the other references noted in the text.

Part III describes a structure; it is an outline of a possible program or way of thinking about and organizing one's recovery. The goal as I have identified it in this book is to actually recover. That means accomplishing what corresponds to that threadbare advice: "Get a life!" One's life is filled with interest, possibility, and the presence of whole worlds of experience and existence. This could be a starting place.

The final part is a series of brief reminders: live in the present, work your own program, trust in the process, and utilize your recovery community.

That's about it. There are volumes on the finer points of gestalt therapy and addictions work. This is not an exhaustive treatment of either. Hopefully it is a significant contribution that will help people think and help therapists work thoughtfully with their clients.

I

The Need to Change

1

The Nature of Addiction and Self-Medicating Behaviors

This chapter addresses the nature of addiction and self-medicating behaviors, and provides working definitions of each. It differentiates between abuse and addiction.

When I meet people to do psychotherapy, I try to focus on that meeting. The focus is not what I want out of the meeting but what the client wants. What does any given person think he or she might accomplish by coming to a therapist? Just as therapists know that therapy is the client's work—that the client must do personal work and work hard to face things previously not faceable—the goal or hope in doing such work must also belong to the client. That is why I try to focus and even re-focus as the work unfolds to make sure the client gets to where he or she wants to go, or for that matter, so that the client begins to realize what he or she actually wants.

Whenever I have asked people what they want in life, many people say they want to be happy. However, only a few know clearly what that means for them. Nevertheless, various psychotherapists would attempt to work with the client to reach the desired goal. A cognitive therapist would explore the way the client thinks in order to detect faulty thinking patterns that disrupt the client's happiness. A relational psychoanalyst would explore the connection between the client and him- or herself under the assumption that the way the client relates to the therapist is the way the client will relate to others, and that relationships, going way back to an infant's first attachment, are the bedrock of happiness. A behaviorist will utilize and multiply the activities and behaviors that bring the client pleasure and shape the client's life through reinforcement. A solutions-focused therapist will fantasize with the client what might make the client happy, and then together they would devise a plan to travel the shortest distance to that goal. A gestalt therapist would establish a meaningful relationship with the client to explore the client's subjective experience of life, how the client makes meaning out of experience, and how the client connects with others in relationships, and to bring to the client's awareness the patterns by which the client does whatever he or she does, trusting the client to make creative adjustments, with increased awareness, that would lead to happiness.

However, none of these approaches is guaranteed to produce happiness.

The psychiatrist and the drug dealer have another answer, though, and that is to alter the brain chemistry: "Take this Valium, and then you'll be less anxious, and perhaps then you will be happy." "Take this lithium, and then you will be less given to mood swings of mania and depression, and then perhaps you will find happiness." "Take this Zoloft and over time your mood will be less depressed; you will be happy." "Smoke this weed." "Sniff this cocaine." Many people who cannot afford prescription drugs self-medicate through the use of street drugs, but these "solutions" are not long-term solutions; at best they manage a given disorder that remains intact. Just as a diabetic must take insulin to maintain metabolic equilibrium, some people with mental disorders must take their medications to stay in balance. But does that make them happy?

> It's about 7:30 pm on the locked unit. People have had their evening meal. Some have settled down to watch television in the group room. Others are sleeping already in their beds.
>
> We used to take people out for cigarette break, but that doesn't happen anymore. Smoking is dangerous to the health, and nicotine is an addictive substance. It makes no sense to advocate a recovery motif, including the non-support for addictive substances—but then to support smoking. Although it is annoying to have to fend off the complaining and whining about not being able to smoke, no staff members want to escort the patients onto the landing and stand in their midst while they smoke, nor for that matter to deal with them when they beg for a second cigarette. Inside, nobody looks at the methadone being handed out. As with the nicotine, we don't want to think too deeply about supporting one habit while complaining about another.

Occasionally, people are admitted for treatment precisely because they have become addicted to medication that has been prescribed in an entirely legal fashion.

Some are addicted to analgesics (pain medication); what started out as a natural response to back injury or surgery obtained a power of its own. The morphine (also known as MS Contin), meperidine (Demerol), oxycodone or oxycontin, or hydrocodone (Vicodin) assumed control. The pain sufferer developed tolerance, became dependent, and then realized he or she had become addicted.

Others are addicted to anxiolytics (antianxiety medications). The alprazolam (also known as Xanax), chlordiazepoxide (Librium), clonazepam (Klonopin), clorazepate (Tranxene), diazepam (Valium), or lorazepam (Ativan), and the sedatives such as amobarbital (Amytal), pentobarbital (Nembutal), secobarbital (Seconal), or tuinal (which is a combination of amobarbital and secobarbital) that they are prescribed obtained powers of their own. An anxiety-prone person, often unable to sleep at night, first found relief and ability to rest at night and then developed dependence and tolerance, and became addicted.

What is happening in a person who uses some kind of substance or repetitive and compulsive behavior to make him- or herself happy, to overcome bad feelings, or to attempt to manage something that has become unmanageable? At what point in the process does that person become addicted? What is addiction? What does it mean to self-medicate?

DEFINITIONS

The constructs of "addiction" and "self-medicating behaviors" overlap. For some people and in contexts of discussion they refer to the same thing. On the one hand, a very strict understanding of addiction requires physiological dependence upon one or more illegal drugs (DiClemente, 2003), tolerance, and withdrawal. On the other hand, a wider understanding identifies addiction as being anything in which people are consumed with behavior that becomes centrifugal in nature, that is, forcing other parts of life to the periphery of living (Alexander & Schweighofer, 1988).

Some people believe that an addiction is apparent when there is a loss of control over the use of a substance or the repetition of behavior, and continued use of this substance or behavior persists in spite of negative consequences and attempts to quit (Henderson, 2000). In such cases, one's life becomes unmanageable, and the addicted person faces unwanted consequences that result from the overuse in question (Matzko, 2007). It is as if the substance or the behavior has control of the person rather than the person making choices and choosing to use or behave in a certain way. Indeed, this is the assertion of step one in the now classic list of twelve steps used in many treatment approaches (Alcoholics Anonymous, 2002).

Self-medicating behaviors are soothing in nature; they include features of addiction, but they are primarily relieving and psychologically reinforcing. They can include eating, sex, drugs, spending or shopping, and gambling. When self-medicating overlaps addiction, behaviors can include substance abuse, internet addiction, and co-occurring issues such as eating disorders and compulsive gambling. (Wilson, 2010; Young & de Abreu, 2011; Slutske, Piasecki, Blaszczynksi, & Martin, 2010).

Gorski (1989) claimed that addiction includes the effects of the substance and the way in which the addicted person thinks about using or behaving. The thinking problem includes irrational thoughts, unmanageable feelings, and self-defeating behaviors; consequently, the cognitive category alone (the way a person thinks about the substance) is inadequate to address what is actually a whole-person process, but Gorski's observation that addiction is a matter of the effects of the substance and the way in which the person orients to the substance is useful.

Carlo DiClemente (2003) claimed that there are three critical dimensions to addiction: (1) the development of a well-established and problematic pattern of using a substance or self-medicating that is pleasurable and reinforcing, (2) physiological and psychological features that constitute dependence, and (3) the interaction of these things that makes the behavior in question resistant to change. The term dependence shows that

> the pattern of behavior involves poor self-regulatory control, continues despite negative feedback, and often appears to be out of control...
>
> ...failure to change, despite the outward appearance that change would be both possible and in the best interest of the individual, is considered a cardinal characteristic in defining addictions.
>
> (DiClemente, 2003, p. 4)

The journey from use to abuse and then to dependency is "related to the person's capacity to interact with others and his or her ability to tolerate sensations such as frustration, anger, and fear" (Clemmens & Matzko, 2005). The addictive and the self-medicating character of these behaviors become so recurrent and habitual that they constitute a procedure in living. Addiction and self-medicating behaviors are the first options an addict turns to under virtually any kind of stimulation (Clemmens, 1997, 2005); it is what he or she does as a way of life. Addiction absorbs elements of a person's horizon, reducing potentialities and possibilities to a small repertoire of options.

Another way of understanding addiction and self-medication is to comprehend the larger contexts, what gestalt therapists call the field (or fields), in which they occur. More will be said about field dynamics in a subsequent chapter, but at this point it is enough to say that addictive behaviors are complex disorders that develop through multiple processes that are biological, cognitive, psychological, and sociocultural in nature (Donovan, 2005). Thus, addiction and self-medicating are never one-person processes, as if the problem belongs to the addict alone. They always involve other people even though the addict or self-medicating person remains responsible as the agent of behavior for whom the use of a substance or the use of some kind of action serves some purpose. Addiction and self-medicating behaviors are functional and relational.

This brings to mind the differences among various constructs when thinking about addiction and self-medicating. Some view addiction as a disease, and in that case one either has the disease or one does not, regardless of how much or how little one uses medication. The first journal dedicated to the addiction issue was the *Quarterly Journal of Inebriety* (JI), which began publishing in 1876. The JI's central proposition was that inebriety (consisting largely of alcohol and opiate consumption) was a disease, and that position was greeted by opposition, criticism, condemnation, and denunciation. Most of these reactions were from religious leaders, who viewed the journal as one excusing crime and vice (Weiner & White, 2007).

Others view addiction and self-medicating on a continuum of behaviors. On such a continuum, one might find lesser or greater examples of a given dynamic. Figure 1.1 provides an example of such a continuum. One could be said to have the "disease" at the addiction end of the continuum but not necessarily to have it at the intoxication end. One could say that the social user who is not dependent does not have the disease, but that the addicted user, who may or may not be intoxicated at any given time, has it. Further, the issue of self-medicating can be seen to inhabit a "no-man's-land" between these two extremes. In some cases, self-medicating is just one feature of an addiction, while in others it is not part of an addiction at all. In some cases a person either chooses not to stop drinking or cannot stop drinking, but the drinking in question does not cause problems in the person's life and he or

Intoxication–Abuse–Dependence

Social Use–Self-Medication–Addiction

FIGURE 1.1 Continuum of Use and Addiction

she does not exhibit tolerance. Discerning the way in which any given person manifests abuse, self-medicating, dependence, tolerance, and addiction requires an appreciation of complexity and the capacity to engage in critical thinking (Taleff, 2006).

A CLOSER LOOK AT SELF-MEDICATING

Self-medicating can refer, literally, to using a substance as if it were medication—taking a substance so that it will somehow ameliorate unwanted or uncomfortable experience. For instance, a person can drink alcohol to enhance the sedative effect of a prescribed medication. A person can smoke marijuana to blunt anxiety or use cocaine to overcome social awkwardness. It is a covering up of one kind of experience with another. It is a dissipation of one kind of experience with another. Thus, it can also refer to action that distracts or covers up actions such as yelling angrily at one's partner after learning that one's performance review at work left one's job security in doubt. The purpose of self-medicating is to make bad feelings go away, and people can do that by using a substance but also by engaging in various behaviors, both of which have a biochemical effect in one's brain and a relational impact on one's social life.

Often, the dynamics of self-medicating are learned in the intergenerational structures of one's family relationships. In alcoholic, dysfunctional families, children learn a codependent coping strategy (Scaturo, 2005; Beesley & Stoltenberg, 2002), grow up having to deal with an alcoholic parent, and tell themselves that when they get free—when they grow up themselves—they will never drink. Then, they realize several years down the road that they get by in life by overworking, spending, eating, sexual activities, relationships, gambling, or excessive anger in rage—all behaviors utilized when life circumstances deal out discouragement, stress, loss, or other reminders of the pain they had to go through when they set their childhoods aside to serve the needs of their parents. Even if one did not grow up in a dysfunctional family, he or she can enter into a codependent relationship—"a relationship based on a bond of suffering and conflict with a person who is physically or emotionally incapacitated and does nothing to solve his or her problem" (Noriega, Ramos, Nedina-Mora, & Villa, 2008, p. 208). In such an instance, the "person maintains a low self-esteem, remains unhappy, yet wishes and seeks fulfillment. Compulsions and addictions ('repetition compulsions') can provide temporary fulfillment, but lead to more suffering...What results from the above described wounding process is co-dependence in its primary form." (Whitfield, 1993, pp. 58–59)

Thus, self-medicating is a common feature of addiction, whether it is in the behavior of the primarily incapacitated individual or the person codependently related. Beattie (2009) reflected on the phenomenon, saying, "Codependency is subtle, insidious. To recover from chemical dependency, we admit that we're powerless over alcohol. We realize we aren't controlling alcohol; it's controlling us. Now alcohol was controlling me again, but it was the alcohol *someone else* was drinking." (p. 66)

DIFFERENTIATING BETWEEN ABUSE AND ADDICTION

The *Diagnostic and Statistical Manual of Mental Disorders*, 4th edition, with text revision (APA, 2000), differentiates between substance abuse and substance dependence. While substance abuse is characterized by the use that is risky and that causes disruptions and problems in a person's life, dependence is characterized by the use that is abusive in nature and includes tolerance, withdrawal, and compulsive use in spite of attempts to quit or reduce frequency or amount of use.

More specifically, substance abuse is defined as maladaptive behavior in patterns of substance use that manifest "recurrent and significant adverse consequences related to the repeated use..." (APA, 2000, p. 198) in which any one or more of the following can be seen within any given twelve-month period of time and the conditions for substance dependence have not been met: (1) recurring use that results in failure to fulfill obligations in the various contexts of life (such as work or school); (2) recurring use in which physical risk (such as driving while impaired) is present; (3) recurring substance-related legal problems; (4) continued use in spite of repetitive social or interpersonal problems that are direct consequences of repeated use.

More specifically, also, substance dependence is defined as cognitive, behavioral, and physical characteristics, showing that a person continues to use a substance in spite of the fact that it causes a great deal of difficulty and that three or more of the following can be seen during any given 12-month period: (1) tolerance (the need for increasing quantities of the substance to achieve intoxication or the desired experience); (2) withdrawal (cognitive and physiological behavior change resulting from declining levels of a given substance in the blood or body tissues in people who had maintained heavy dosage over time); (3) compulsive use, either by taking more doses over a longer period of time than originally intended and/or continuing to use in spite of a desire to reduce or discontinue using; (4) so much time is spent in the rituals of obtaining or using the substance that using pushes to the side the other aspects of life, even important social, occupational, and personally significant people and activities; (5) in spite of the mounting damage and loss accruing through the use of the substance, the person in question continues to use. The key element is that even in the face of this accruing loss, and even when the person admits that he or she ought to quit and wants to quit, the use continues.

CONTRASTING SCENARIOS

Consider the following examples. People like these can be found in most places. These people are fictional characters, but they exhibit characteristics present in real persons.

Lisa

Lisa was a young woman of 27. She had dark, straight hair, was slender, and she liked to dress sharply in dark colors. That was difficult for her in Bermuda where the heat, humidity, and sunshine of summer keep people in light colored, casual shorts. She came from a working-class family in Canada, and she was privileged to have completed her university education. In that regard, she was the pride of her parents, and she felt a bit of a burden to make good in life and to achieve both financial and personal stability. She could work hard, and she was beginning to realize that there were some benefits to playing hard as well.

She was not afraid to show her skin a little in order to attract attention. She had had two boyfriends when she was in Bermuda. Both relationships had faded away in an unsatisfying fashion.

Lisa worked for an exempt company in Bermuda, crunching numbers as an accountant. She had done well in math while in school, and she realized that certified accountants could make their way nicely in the world, often working in diverse locations. She wanted to travel; so, she had accepted a job, moved to the island with little baggage, and she considered it all an adventure.

Not long after coming to Bermuda, Lisa realized that if she wanted to meet people, it would have to be in one of the clubs because leisure activities centered around club social life and water sports, but she neither owned a boat nor knew anyone who owned a boat. She opted for the clubs, and she began going to happy hour at the Pickled Onion, Latin, and the Hamilton Princess. The drinks were exotic. The atmosphere was hilarious and exciting. She found herself attracted to it. She liked it, and she also found herself liking the way alcohol made her feel.

It was not long before Lisa was going for longer lunches and having a couple of drinks during the day while gone. One day she came back to the office and people could smell the alcohol on her body. She was intoxicated, which on the one hand was just fine with her because she didn't want to feel any pain, but on the other, it was dangerous, if not reckless. She'd been lonely because she had dated several men but not found one that resulted in a satisfying, long-term relationship. She did not like to think about getting older and not having someone; so, forgetting about all that and feeling "good" with a drink or two seemed to make sense. However, that day she had had a little too much. Her speech was slightly slurred and when she came back to the office she was unsteady on her feet.

Her coworkers were aghast. They picked her up and ushered her out of the building, explaining to the supervisor that Lisa must have eaten something bad at lunch. They took her to her home and told her to sleep it off.

This kind of behavior continued. Lisa's performance began to slip. Eventually, her supervisor talked to her about the lack of quality in her work, the numerous mistakes she was making, and her frequent sick days off work. He questioned if she had a "drinking problem" and suggested she go for counseling at the EAP.

This performance review, however, did not affect her drinking habits. Lisa did not think she had a problem with alcohol. She knew exactly why she was drinking, and she believed she could keep doing it or even stop whenever she wanted. She chose simply not to drink at lunch anymore, which lasted for about two weeks before she gave herself a gift and had a glass of wine. She told herself that just one glass of wine at lunch could not hurt, and that is where she kept it, but her consumption after work remained what it had become at her peak. She was becoming intoxicated to the point of not remembering the evening at least two times each week. Her consumption was eating up her funds so that the money that she told herself she could make and save as a result of working in Bermuda was being poured down her throat each night during happy hour. The more she drank, the less attractive she became, and the less attractive she became, the more lonely life seemed to be. The situation was going downhill.

Gilbert and Melissa

Gilbert preferred to be called "Gil." He was 28 years old and had grown up in Bermuda. His parents had sent him to private school, which is what any family of means does in Bermuda, because the public schools do not compete. At sixteen years of age, he was on the "bike," which is what motorized scooters are called on the island. At sixteen, Bermudian adolescents obtain a rite of passage by getting a driver's license and a bike of their own, and with the increased freedom and apparent independence usually also comes drinking, drugging, and sexual activity. "Apparent" is the correct word in this context because actually it is so expensive to live in Bermuda that adolescents rarely move out on their own before becoming thoroughly ensconced in a successful career, and that follows some time away at the university. Gil attended Dalhousie University in Halifax, Nova Scotia, and got a Bachelor of Commerce degree with a major in business management. At one point, he thought he might stay and complete a MBA, but his parents wanted him to return to the island and start working.

When Gil was in school, he met a Canadian girl, Melissa, who had grown up in Cape Breton. She was a country girl whose parents had been devoted to natural foods and the traditional Gaelic music popular there. Melissa was the oldest of four children, and she was used to taking care of her siblings while both of her parents worked and devoted themselves to music, step dancing, and attending one ceilidh or another, time after time. Gil, and the lure of living on a subtropical island, captured her imagination, and the two set up house with one another, marrying just before Gil returned to the island.

Gil had been drinking and drugging since high school. He did not stop while at Dalhousie, and Melissa knew about it, but she considered his use to be small scale and expected it to vanish after college when it was time to settle down. However, when he returned to Bermuda and got work as an insurance underwriter, Gil was pleased to learn that quite a lot of business was written through lunches and dinners that included lubricating the deals with alcohol. Although he also smoked marijuana, he preferred feeling a few drinks under his belt.

Over time his consumption of alcohol increased dramatically. He began to pride himself in being able to "hold" his liquor, and he could down increasing amounts of beer, rum, and vodka without feeling intoxicated. There were times people had to bring him home and Melissa had to put him to bed drunk, but it was not much of a concern because he did not remember how he had gotten home. There were times when he had to call in "sick" because he had been too drunk the night before, and the night before had simply blended into the day after. There were also days when his hangover was too debilitating, and Melissa had to call in and tell his job that he was too ill to come in that day.

Melissa grew lonely in Bermuda. It was nothing like home for her. She wilted in the summer heat even though at first she relished the sun, the pink sand, the warm water, and the beaches. Gil was gone most of the time, and with the downturn in the economy, Melissa had not been able to find a job. She was bored. She felt neglected, and when Gil stayed out late drinking with his friends and business associates, she felt hurt. To compensate, she told herself she deserved to play as well, and so she began buying clothes online and had them shipped to herself in Bermuda. It was taking money out of their accounts that they had been saving to eventually purchase a place of their own, but she could not stop. It was the only thing she had.

After three years of rough living, Gil decided to quit drinking. The trouble was that a day later he became depressed, distracted, could not sleep well at night because of nightmares, and his hands began trembling. That tremble invaded his voice, and he felt fragile. His condition preyed on Melissa's mind, and she told him to get some help. He could not think straight. He complained to her, "Oh great. Just when I try to quit drinking, I have to come down with the flu," and he started to feel anxious and worried whether he would be able to go to work again.

She told him, "I don't think this is the flu."

It was not the flu, and the symptoms vanished as soon as he started drinking again. He told himself he would gradually decrease the amount he was drinking, but that also did not work. He realized he was caught on a treadmill of alcohol consumption and the speed was too fast to do anything but keep running. Everything he did seemed to include drinking or actually centered on drinking. The thought of doing something that did not include alcohol was simply not on his horizon.

CONCLUSION

Lisa is an example of substance abuse. Gil is an example of substance dependence, and Melissa is an example of codependent self-medication. Actually, self-medicating as a dynamic can be found in all three of them.

Addiction is a common term, and most people believe they know what it means. However, for an addiction to exist, someone must engage in substance use or compulsive behavior that is pleasurable and physiologically and/or psychologically rewarding and that fosters dependence and withdrawal and resists limiting or discontinuation. It is to be distinguished from substance abuse, which is the repeated use of a substance that is risky and/or results in some kind of loss of function, status, or benefit.

According to a popular idiom, people are not "cured" of addiction— once an addict, always an addict; but people can "recover" from an addictive lifestyle. Just what recovery is and the role therapists can play in a person's recovery is the subject of the next chapter.

REFERENCES AND RESOURCES

Alcoholics Anonymous (2002) *Twelve Steps and Twelve Traditions.* New York: Alcoholics Anonymous World Services, Inc.

Alexander, A. & Schweighofer, A. (1988) Defining "addiction." *Canadian Psychology/Psychologie Canadienne,* 29(2), 151–162.

American Psychiatric Association (2000) *Diagnostic and Statistical Manual of Mental Disorders, 4th edition, Text Revision.* Washington, DC: American Psychiatric Association.

Beattie, M. (2009) *The New Codependency: Help and Guidance for Today's Generation.* New York: Simon & Schuster.

Beesley, D. & Stoltenberg, C. (2002) Control, attachment style, and relationship satisfaction among adult children of alcoholics. *Journal of Mental Health Counseling,* 24(4), 281–298.

Clemmens, M. (2005) *Getting Beyond Sobriety: Clinical Approaches to Long-Term Recovery.* Cambridge, MA: Gestalt Press.

Clemmens, M. (1997) *Getting beyond Sobriety: Clinical Approaches to Long-Term Recovery.* San Francisco, CA: Jossey-Bass.

Clemmens, M. & Matzko, H. (2005) Gestalt approaches to substance use/abuse/dependency: Theory and practice. In A. Woldt & S. Toman (Eds.) *Gestalt Therapy History, Theory, and Practice* (pp. 279–300) Thousand Oaks, CA: Sage Publications.

DiClemente, C. (2003) *Addiction and Change: How Addictions Develop and Addicted People Recover.* NewYork: The Guilford Press

Donovan, D. (2005) Assessment of addictive behaviors for relapse prevention. In D. Donovan & G. Marlatt (Eds.) *Assessment of Addictive Behaviors* (pp. 1–48). New York: The Guilford Press.

Gorski, T. (1989) *Passages through Recovery: An Action Plan for Preventing Relapse.* Center City, MN: Hazelden.

Henderson, E. (2000) *Understanding Addiction.* Jackson, MS: University of Mississippi.

Matzko, H. (2007) *Addiction, Resistance, Forgiveness & Treatment: a Clinician's Guide to Addiction Treatment from the Perspective of a Gestalt Therapist.* Cranston, RI: Gestalt Institute of Rhode Island.

Noriega, G., Ramos, L., Medina-Mora, M.aE., & Villa, A. (2008) Prevalence of codependence in young women seeking primary health: Care and associated risk factors. *American Journal of Orthopsychiatry*, 78(2), 199–210

Scaturo, D. (2005) Family therapy: Dilemmas of codependency and family homeostasis. In D. Scaturo (author) *Clinical Dilemmas in Psychotherapy: a Transtheoretical Approach to Psychotherapy Integration* (pp. 99–110). Washington, DC: American Psychological Association.

Slutske, W., Piasecki, T., Blaszczynski, A., & Martin, N. (2010) Pathological gambling recovery in the absence of abstinence. *Addiction*, 105(12), 2169–2175.

Taleff, M. (2006) *Critical Thinking for Addiction Professionals*. New York: Springer Publishing.

Weiner, B. & White, W. (2007) The Journal of Inebriety (1876–1914): History, topical analysis, and photographic images. *Addiction*, 102, 15–23.

Whitfield, C. (1993) *Boundaries and Relationships: Knowing, Protecting and Enjoying the Self*. Deefield Beach, FL: Health Communications, Inc.

Wilson, G. (2010) Eating disorders, obesity and addiction. *European Eating Disorders Review*, 18(5), 341–351.

Young, K. & de Abreu, C., eds. (2011) Internet addiction: *A handbook and guide to evaluation and treatment*. Hoboken, NJ: John Wiley & Sons, Inc.

2

Just How Fixed Can One Get?
The Nature of Recovery

*This chapter addresses the nature of recovery, providing a
working definition. It addresses models of recovery, and it
covers programs of recovery. It also addresses the issue of the
effectiveness of treatment for addiction.*

It is evening on the locked unit. Supper is over, and the trays have
been put back on the meal cart. The meal cart has been taken away.
It's time for evening group. This one will be on relapse prevention, specifically a psychoeducational group on the relapse cycle. Some of the
patients have been here before, and they could almost recite the script
as well as the staff member who leads the group.

The staff member opens the group by saying, "Welcome everyone.
This is relapse prevention group, and tonight we're going to talk about
how the relapse cycle fits into a person's recovery."

A young man, unshaven, wearing dirty pajamas, says, "What would
you know about *my* recovery?"

The staff person says, "Recovery of course is your work, and each
one of you has your own passage of recovery to navigate." Under his
breath he says to himself, "... but this place is not a bus stop on your
journey of self-help. I'm not here as a passive piece of some kind of
recovery puzzle. You don't simply use me to recover. I have something
to contribute to you in the process, and I have knowledge about what
addiction is, how it works, and how people can best help themselves
to remain sober. As an addiction specialist, I can help facilitate your
recovery."

"Okay, okay," says the young man in the pajamas. "Get on with it then."

The others in the group settle back as if to watch a movie, and the staff member draws a clock on the chalkboard. He is off on his well-learned talk about how the experience of relapse typically takes place and how the relapse cycle fits into any given person's recovery.

All of this begs the question of just what recovery is. Is recovery a construct based in self-help or is it something professionals can use as well in their work with addicted and self-medicating clients? The answer is that "recovery" is a term that has entered the general idiom to such an extent it can be used by professionals as well. The public has a general idea of what it means. To the public it means getting beyond and overcoming an addiction. Because most 12-step programs use the concept of recovery, patients encounter the term when they enroll in residential treatment for addiction. They continue to see it among the other patients at their weekly meetings. Therefore, it is wise for professionals working with addicted people to have a clear understanding of what those people mean when they use the term, for use it they will. Every substance abuse counselor will inevitably find him- or herself also using the term while dealing with clients.

MODELS OF RECOVERY

The word "recovery" is compatible with the disease model of addiction. If one has a bacterial infection, one has to follow directions, take the antibiotics, and wait to recover. One has to follow the doctor's advice, and then recovery takes place. One gets well. If one has a chronic illness, however, one never quite "gets well;" one has to manage a condition that more or less remains ever present.

In this model, with this kind of language about getting well, one has to decide to follow the doctor's advice; so, although a person might say he or she has contracted a chronic disease, he or she still must decide to follow the advice and practice the disciplines inherent to the given recovery regimen. That is what it takes to manage a chronic illness.

Any time you make a decision, you say "yes" to one thing and "no" to another. If you decide to get up and go for a walk before breakfast, you say yes to exercise and you say no to staying in bed and getting some more sleep. Often choosing one thing means saying no to several other options. A person looking for a job receives five offers, and he or she has to choose one. A person faced with several courses of action, all of which might be considered healthy or recovery oriented, must choose one at any given time and at least say "not now" to the others.

We may have several thoughts vying for attention, but we can only scrutinize one at a time. Such decision making calls for executive functions of sorting and choosing according to priorities.

To do this in an organized way focused on a particular activity or concern is to be disciplined. A discipline can be a branch of learning, but discipline itself is activity or experience that provides mental or physical training. Put another way, a discipline is something one does. A person does not wait until he or she feels like doing it. One just does it, and although a discipline can be enjoyable in itself, one usually takes a disciplined approach out of a sense that such activity is essential toward some other goal. If a person is a disciplined runner, he or she runs. If a person is disciplined in his or her thoughts, that person practices logical thought patterns and puts thinking through rigorous tests to make sure his or her thoughts and conclusions make sense. If a person is disciplined in eating, he or she does not simply diet to lose weight, then go off the diet and put the weight back on. That person changes his or her lifestyle by the discipline one applies to nutrition, and eats what is good as a way of life. Thus, that person does not put the weight back on but keeps it off because he or she has made a lifestyle change.

All of that is what working a "program" of recovery is like.

PROGRAMS OF RECOVERY

People who enroll in residential treatment programs for addiction do more than simply learn a vocabulary and a few concepts related to sobriety. They begin practicing disciplines, and they begin disciplining themselves in the various aspects of their program. A program of recovery is not simply a self-help gimmick; it includes professional addiction specialists working with clients over a period of time, a scenario that resembles athletes in training. Furthermore, people in recovery do not succeed by running sprints or dashes; they must endure long distances. Indeed, the endurance race of recovery only *begins* in residential treatment; it must continue and be adapted to the specific needs of each person once that person emerges from residential treatment and reenters his or her home world.

Counselors, therapists, and psychologists can facilitate the working of such recovery programs by either helping their addicted clients create a personal program of recovery from the ground up or by adapting a program learned in a residential treatment center after the clients have returned to their lives in any given place. This focus and understanding of what the work of therapy will be about needs to be part of the basic contracting between therapist and client (Mann, 2010), so that although therapy will uncover unexpected patterns—and although there needs to be flexibility enough to develop awareness in unexpected directions—the overall goal of developing a recovery program is understood from the beginning and does not get lost.

Gestalt therapists can be especially helpful in this kind of recovery work, because they are equipped by praxis to explore patterns in the client's situation, personal experience, and relational patterns that support either addiction or recovery. Together with the client, gestalt therapists can facilitate a growing awareness of critical factors relevant to the client's unique needs and program of recovery.

Having a recovery program does not mean the client simply adopts someone else's idea of how he or she ought to live. In fact, to leave it at that is to attempt to live one's life with a paint-by-numbers approach that never becomes one's own, relevant approach—an approach that can't stand the test of time in the real world. Every person needs to have a program that fits him or her. That is why those coming back from residential treatment do well to find an outpatient therapist who is adept at addictions work and who can help them with the transition. Without this transition, and without the adjustments necessary to make a one-size-fits-all program into one's own, unique plan, going to "rehab" turns out to be nothing more than going on a diet. The addict usually just "puts the weight back on" (i.e., relapses, after a short while).

Whenever someone chooses recovery over addiction as a way of life, they are choosing recovery *from* and/or recovery *to*. That is, at any given time in recovery, a person is either oriented toward the past from which he or she is attempting to recover or oriented toward the present (and then of course the future in which he or she is attempting to live more productively). People in recovery are attempting to escape a life of addiction or to grasp hold of life itself, to LIVE, to *get a life*. This chapter describes the recovery movement and contrasts two views of recovery: recovery *from* the negative spiral of self-medicating behaviors and recovery *to* a positive hope and direction—from ruination to reconstruction. Thus, the view of recovery advocated here is not just about sobriety; it is about overall health and well-being, what Michael Clemmens (1997) called, "getting beyond sobriety."

A WORKING DEFINITION OF RECOVERY

The construct of recovery is both a name for a process and a reference for a movement. When seen through the lens of the movement, one most often encounters self-help literature. When seen through the lens of a process, one considers growth and change that occurs in people, and that process quite often includes the work of addiction profession-als. In reality, the construct of recovery has become all but synonymous for addictions work (Weiner & White, 2001), but it also applies to prog-ress with regard to any number of psychopathologies or neurological maladies (Bradshaw et al., 2011; Kidd et al., 2011; Warren, 2011).

The process of recovery includes many factors and is not in itself anti-thetical to treatment for addiction. In fact, treatment for addiction con-tributes to recovery. In a study of evidence-based practice in a substance abuse treatment program conducted at Texas Christian University, stages of recovery were correlated to operational and organizational dynamics in implementing treatment (Lehman, Simpson, Knight, & Flynn, 2011). It is a false dichotomy to regard "recovery" as one thing, positioned at one end of a continuum between self-help and treatment, and therapy as something else positioned at the other end. Thus, psychotherapists and substance abuse counselors can be instrumental to the client's recovery, and "recovery" can be a useful construct in the process of therapy.

Abstinence is simply sobriety, the presence of the absence of using an addictive substance or engaging in compulsive self-medicating behaviors. Recovery, however, is a freely chosen lifestyle character-ized by sobriety, health, and responsible participation in one's social world; it is the absence of mood-altering substances and the mainte-nance of a program designed for growth in the person and enhance-ment of the person's life (Hanley, Ganley, & Carducci, 2008). In a study (Laudet, 2007) investigating how people in recovery define the term, most indicated that recovery involved total abstinence, but they also stipulated that recovery went past abstinence and was experienced as an abundant new life, a continuous growth process of self-change, and a reclaiming of one's self.

There are three main stages in recovery-related treatment:

1. *The detoxification or stabilization stage of care* usually occurs in an inpatient setting, is several days in duration, and is focused on ame-liorating the physiological and emotional symptoms that follow recent substance use and motivating the patient to accept that there is a prob-lem and to learn how to deal with that problem.

2. *The intermediate stage of care* sometimes occurs in a residential setting but usually occurs in an outpatient setting, is several weeks or months in duration, and is focused on teaching the patient new skills to cope with relapse situations and motivating him or her to develop and maintain lifestyle changes that are inconsistent with substance use.

3. *The continuing care stage of treatment is* one or more years in dura-tion and focused on relapse prevention through continued support

of positive lifestyle changes and regular monitoring of potential risk factors for return to substance use.

(Adapted from McLellan, 2003)

This construct of the experience of self is important. Many spiritual approaches to recovery advocate letting go and getting God, losing oneself in order to find oneself. This sounds good, and it seems spiritually proper. However, one must first *have* a self in order to set one's self aside. One must have a strong sense of what it feels like to be a person—the subjective, first-person experience of being alive and grounded in a world, in order to make the deliberate and strong choice of yielding one's self to a higher power. More will be said about this later in another chapter.

EFFECTIVENESS

The various treatments associated with recovery have been found to be effective (Mee-Lee, McLellan, & Miller, 2010). Treatment for substance abuse and dependence has been shown to be conducive for recovery across racial and gender lines (Godley, Hedges, & Hunter, 2011). Factors contributing to long-term recovery, where recovery is considered a lifelong process, are such things as social and community support, affiliation with 12-step organizations, negative consequences of substance use (Laudet, Savage, & Mahmood, 2002), mental health (Webb, Robinson, & Bower, 2011), and motivation (DiClemente, Kofeldt, & Gemmell, 2011). There is some evidence that addicted people, after having moved through the phases of recovery, can experience greater quality of life than before they became addicted (Hibbert & Best, 2011), which bodes well for the positive effects of a recovery program.

When the state of Connecticut implemented a recovery-oriented model for its entire public/private health care system, it saw a 62% decrease in acute care use, 14% lower cost, 40% increase in first-time admissions, and 24% decrease in average annual cost per client (Kirk, 2011). Indeed, patients with severe psychological disorders do well when their treatment assumes a recovery motif.

Although Hazelden points to very positive outcomes over the first year following treatment,[1] traditionally, outcomes linked to complete sobriety have been mediocre, showing that about 50% of addicted people return to their drug of choice within the first 6 months of post-residential treatment (Mee-Lee et al., 2010). Overall outcomes for dominant acute care programs could be better, and that is because there is a mismatch between the chronic needs of addicted people and the terminal nature of such programs. The follow-up and management of recovery need to be a matter of concern just as seriously as the residential, detox programs that focus on achieving initial sobriety (Kelly & White, 2011).[2]

For instance, the therapeutic use of relapse is an important consideration in management of recovery, but relapse in residential treatment is usually considered failure. When percentage of days sober is used as a benchmark instead of continuous days abstinent, then two things follow. The therapist and client begin to use the experience of relapse as a way to understand the process of recovery more completely, and the client has less need to work his or her way through the shame and the disappointment of having "failed," finding him- or herself back at square one. The approach in such cases is often client driven (with the therapist focusing and clarifying for the client figures of interest and practical goals) and can be informed by the progress the client makes along several dimensional scales. Rather than a categorical approach in which the client is either sober or not sober, the client can be seen to be "in process" and making progress. The approach advocated in this book deviates from the "days sober" approach found in 12-step programs and falls into line with the client-driven approach identified as especially conducive to positive outcomes and evidence-based practice; it "begins with the outcome the client desires" (Mee-Lee et al., 2010, p. 206). In this approach, a dialogical relationship is used along with a phenomenological tracking of the client's experience to keep constant with emerging nuances in the client's purposes. Make no mistake, I find 12-step programs helpful and supportive, but not everything in them is equally beneficial.

LISA, GIL, AND MELISSA

Lisa was sent to the Employee Assistance Program (EAP) on a formal referral by her supervisor. The counselor introduced himself, and proceeded to give Lisa the informed consent document that he usually provides to each client in the first meeting. He told her that the formal nature of this referral meant that he would be reporting back to her supervisor on the status of their work, attendance at sessions, and progress made. He told her that he was a gestalt therapist, and he described the main principles in gestalt therapy that he would use in their work together. He told her a little about his background, and he asked her if she had any questions or concerns.

She said, "No."

He asked, "What is your understanding of why you are here? Why did they send you to EAP?"

Lisa said, "I don't know."

"You mean right now, at this instant, you don't even know why you are here?"

"Well, my supervisor told me he thought I was an alcoholic."

"Wow. That seems like quite an accusation."

"I know! I don't think I'm an alcoholic."

"I notice when you said that, there was a little emotion in your voice."

Lisa's lip quivered. She turned her eyes to the floor. "Like, yeah. My mother was an alcoholic," she said, "and I'm not anything like her!"

"You're not an alcoholic?"

"No."

"You're not like your mother?"

"No!"

"Help me understand, then. What would make your supervisor take you away from your work, tell you he thought you were an alcoholic, and send you over to meet with me?"

"He said I should discuss it with you, but he didn't tell me anything else."

"What's it like to have people think you're an alcoholic?"

"Look, I do drink. I'm not going to say that I don't. But I can control it. One time I got really drunk at a lunch and my friends had to take me home; so, now I just have one glass of wine at lunch. It's no big deal."

"Your supervisor indicated that you had numerous days off sick and that your work performance had gone down. He said you'd been seen quite intoxicated in the evenings during the week."

She did not answer, and she did not look happy.

The therapist asked, "Lisa, what do you want to accomplish by coming here?"

She answered, "I'd like to get my supervisor to leave me alone."

The therapist continued, "Okay. That sounds like something we might be able to accomplish. I can't tell if you are an alcoholic or not, but if you're up for it, we could do an experiment and see what happens. You up for that?"

Lisa asked, "What kind of experiment?"

"Well, let's see you not use any alcohol at all for six weeks."

Lisa said, "Why should I do that? I like having a drink once in a while, and I already told you I could control it."

"Right. This is not a forever thing. You said you could control it. In my experience of working with people, many people believe they can control it. Would you be willing to test how much control you really have over it, and in the process perhaps prove to yourself and your supervisor that you do have control over it?"

Lisa thought about it for a moment, and then she said, "Yes. I'll do that."

"Great," said the therapist. "How about we check in with this in two weeks. That okay with you?"

She agreed. They set another appointment, and he gave her contact information in case she needed to talk before then.

Meanwhile Gil had decided to get some help. He contacted a local therapist who put him in touch with a residential treatment program in the United States, and Gil started getting ready to take a 6-week leave of absence from work. His employer was supportive, but it meant that their household income would be cut considerably until Gil could get back to work full time, and this sent a shiver through Melissa. She started to panic, and Gil made an appointment for the both of them to see a therapist. On the same day Lisa was leaving the therapist's office, Gil and Melissa were coming through the door.

After the informed consent was accomplished, the therapist inquired what had brought them to the office. They looked at one another, and then Gil said, "You go ahead."

Melissa told the story of getting married and moving to Bermuda after college. She said how she had looked for work but had not been able to find any. She started to describe Gil's drinking, but she became guarded. She didn't want to offend Gil, but he interrupted her and blurted out, "Now is not the time to go mum. You've certainly run me into the ground enough at home about it." Then he turned to the therapist, and he said, "I've got a drinking problem. I drink too much, and I can't stop; so, I'm going away to rehab, but now that I've decided to do that, *she* doesn't want me to go."

Melissa sat tensely. She was pressing her thumb into her thigh, and she was looking away from Gil and the therapist. The therapist said, "Melissa, if your thumb could speak, what would it say?"

She laughed, and shook her hand out. "I didn't notice I was doing that. I just don't know what to say." She looked distraught. "He's going away for six weeks and leaving me by myself here. We'll be on reduced income while he's gone. What am I going to do?"

Gil addressed Melissa. He said, "What do you want me to do? You want me to stay here and just keep going the way I've been going? It won't take long before I'll be out of a job altogether. Is that what you want? This is just hopeless!"

Both of them turned to the therapist. He said, "You've got a complex situation that you're dealing with. It's not hopeless, but it's not simple, and it's not easy. Here is what I suggest: you, Gil, complete your residential treatment, and when you get back we can work on putting into practice here in Bermuda what you learn in the States. While you're gone, Melissa, you come by and we'll start working on your part in this situation."

"My part? I'm not the one who's got a drinking problem."
Gil whipped around and scowled at her. "Nice," he said.
"Well I don't."
"No, but let's not talk about how much money you're going through with your shopaholic routine."
The therapist interrupted them. He held up his hand like a stop sign and said, "Let's not do that."
Gil asked, "So, do you think we're a lost cause or can you help us?"

The therapist said, "Research has shown that psychotherapy works, and it has indicated that all the main approaches seem to work equally as well. I cannot guarantee that a positive result will happen for you, or that it will take place within a certain time frame. I am a gestalt therapist. I follow my clients, attempting to help them become more aware of what they are doing and how they are doing it."

They waited for him to say more.
He continued, "We do things in patterns. You have been interacting with one another here in what I imagine is a typical fashion for you…"
They laughed. "Got that right."

…so anyway, you understand that much. My desire is to help you learn even more about that than you've known before, so that you can choose to do something different if you want to. Some of this will involve how you each experience what is happening, the meaning you make out of it, and the meaning you give to what you see your partner doing. You each have a different perspective of the shared situation in which you find yourselves.

Melissa clarified, "So, do I get this right? When he goes away next week, I'm going to start coming to talk with you?"

"Yes."
Melissa said, "What are we going to talk about? Like I said, I don't have the drinking problem."
The therapist said, "You are in a relationship together, and it's all connected."
On the way out, Gil turned to the therapist and asked, "So, there's hope?"

NOTES

1. In a paper available from the Butler Center for Research, dated February, 2011, the authors cited very positive gains when the criteria were percentage of days patients remained abstinent (as opposed to having had no relapse of any kind). They contrasted a baseline of 37.91% to 98.04% at 1 month, 96.22% at 6 months, and 95.33% at 12 months. Available at http://psycnet.apa.org/psycextra/531732011-001.pdf
2. Toward that end, this book provides a way for therapists to work with clients so as to adapt what the clients learn in detox and expand upon it in long-term recovery.

REFERENCES

Bradshaw, J., Chen, L., Saling, M., Fitt, G., Hughes, A., & Dowd, A. (2011). Neurocognitive recovery in smart syndrome: A case report. *Cephalalgia, 31*(3), 372–376.

Clemmens, M. (1997) *Getting beyond sobriety: Clinical approaches to long-term recovery.* San Francisco, CA: Jossey-Bass.

Clemmens, M. (2005) Gestalt approaches to substance use/abuse/dependency: Theory and practice. In A. Woldt & S. Toman (Eds.) *Gestalt therapy: History, theory, and practice,* pp. 279–300. Thousand Oaks, CA: Sage Publications.

DiClemente, C., Kofeldt, M., & Gemmell, L. (2011). Motivational enhancement. In M. Galanter, & H. Kleber (Eds.), *Psychotherapy for the treatment of substance abuse* (pp. 125–152). Arlington, VA: American Psychiatric Publishing, Inc.

Godley, S., Hedges, K., & Hunter, B. (2011). Gender and racial differences in treatment process and outcome among participants in the adolescent community reinforcement approach. *Psychology of Addictive Behaviors, 25*(1), 143–154.

Hanley, M., Ganley, B., & Carducci, C. (2008). Journeys from addiction to recovery. *Research and Theory for Nursing Practice, 22*(4), 256–272.

Hibbert, L., & Best, W. (2011). Assessing recovery and functioning in former problem drinkers at different stages of their recovery journeys. *Drug and Alcohol Review, 30*(1), 12–30.

Kelly, J., & White, W. (2011). Recovery management and the future of addiction treatment and recovery in the USA: Current clinical psychiatry. In J. Kelly, & W. White (Eds.), *Addiction recovery management: Theory, research, and practice, current clinical psychiatry* (pp. 303–316). Totowa, NJ: Humana Press.

Kidd, S., George, L., O'Connell, M., Sylvestre, J., Kirkpatrick, H., Browne, G.,...Davidson, L. (2011). Recovery-oriented service provision and clinical outcomes in assertive community treatment. *Psychiatric Rehabilitation Journal, 34*(3), 194–201.

Kirk, T. (2011) Connecticut's journey to a statewide recovery-oriented healthcare system: Strategies, successes, and challenges. In J. Kelly & W. White (eds.) *Addiction recovery management: Theory, research and practice, Current clinical psychiatry*, pp. 209–234. Totowa, NJ: Human Press.

Laudet, A. (2007). What does recovery mean to you? Lessons from the recovery experience for research and practice. *Journal of Substance Abuse Treatment, 33(3)*, 243–256.

Laudet, A., Savage, R., & Mahmood, D. (2002). Pathways to long-term recovery: A preliminary investigation. *Journal of Psychoactive Drugs, 34*(3), 305–311.

Lehman, W., Simpson, D., Knight, D., & Flynn, P. (2011). Integration of treatment innovation planning and implementation: Strategic process models and organizational challenges. *Psychology of Addictive Behaviors, 1*(1), 1–10.

Mann, D. (2010). *Gestalt therapy: 100 key points and techniques.* London: Routledge, Taylor and Francis Group.

McLellan, T. (2003). The outcomes movement in addiction treatment: Comments and cautions. In J. Sorensen, R. Rawson, J. Guydish, & J. Zseben (Eds.), *Drug abuse treatment through collaboration: Practice and research partnerships that work* (pp. 157–179). Washington, DC: American Psychological Association.

Mee-Lee, D., McLellan, T., Miller S. (2010). What works in substance abuse and dependence treatment. In B. Duncan, S. Miller, B. Wampold, & M. Hubble (Eds.), *The heart and soul of change: Delivering what works in therapy* (2nd ed., pp. 394–417). Washington, DC: American Psychological Association.

Warren, M. (2011). Core processes of psychopathology and recovery: "Does the dodo bird effect have wings?" *Clinical Psychology Review, 31*(2), 189–192.

Webb, J., Robinson, E., & Bower, K. (2011). Mental health, not social support, mediates the forgivenss-alcohol outcome relationship. *Psychology of Addictive Behaviors*, 1–12.

Weiner, B., & White, W. (2001). The history of addiction/recovery-related periodicals in America: Literature as cultural/professional artifact. *Contemporary Drug Problems, 28*(4), 531–557.

3

The Will to Change

This chapter explores motivation. People must reach a point at which they want recovery more than they want to continue in their patterns of ruination. It conducts this exploration in terms of gestalt therapy's understanding of figure/ground relationships, claiming that the will to change must become figure/foreground to the pattern of self-medicating as ground/ background.

MOTIVATION

The classic model of motivation comes from Abraham Maslow's (1954/1987) work on the influence of needs. As he himself described his theory, it is a positive theory of motivation that

> ...is in the functionalist tradition of James and Dewey, and is fused with the holism of Wertheimer, Goldstein, and Gestalt psychology and with the dynamism of Freud, Fromm, Horney, Reich, Jung, and Adler. This integration or synthesis may be called a holistic-dynamic theory. (p. 15)

According to this theory, people are motivated by basic physical needs and guided by homeostasis and appetite. In the whole person any particular basic need tends to have global influence. For instance, a hungry person looks for food and tends to think of paradise as a place with plenty of it; that person organizes around satisfying hunger. As one level of basic needs is met, a higher level of need emerges and becomes dominant. Thus, gratification becomes as important as deprivation because the satisfying of a need dissolves that need and clears the way for the emergence of another. A person who used to be hungry can then start thinking of finding a secure home, being with other people, or having someone to love. Other levels of needs are safety, belongingness and affection, esteem, and self-actualization. Maslow also conceived of cognitive and aesthetic needs in which people are motivated to know, to understand, and to pleasure themselves with beauty. This was Maslow's hierarchy of needs, and Perls, Hefferline, and Goodman (1951) expressed a similar idea, calling the needs "dominances" and pointing to the unfinished/unfulfilled pattern—as in the Zeigarnik effect—as an organizing dynamic in the self-regulation of the organism. The motivation is to complete it, to satisfy the need, and to quench the hunger.

Although Maslow's work on needs became more familiar, Henry Murray (1938) provided a previous orientation to need satisfaction, and thus motivation, in his field-oriented system of needs and presses (Brownell, 2010a). Kurt Lewin (1940) observed that Murray conceived of the context or environment, as perceived by the individual, to be providing a "press" against one's needs; thus, his consideration of needs was situational and based on the organismic and holistic ideas in currency at the time. Of importance here is the fact that he added interest and habit systems to a model already largely influenced by intrapsychic dynamics. The satisfaction of needs and interests in the individual person was seen to be socially and environmentally constructed. This has importance when considering the recovery needs of any addict; these needs are not simply a matter of the individual and his/her intrapsychic, even intraphysical/bodily, needs. They come into being as part of the larger field, the social context, and they must be understood and dealt with as interpersonally nonindependent. Murray also identified needs for achievement that have been correlated to the midlevel needs in Maslow's hierarchy (Conroy, Elliot, &Thrash, 2009; Cunningham, Wakefield, & Ward, 1975).

Having established that whole-person needs and interests are basic to motivation, there is a prior question that begins to loom large. What is this thing called motivation? Motivation is a teleological construct in that its focus is on a result—a desired result. The *telos is the purpose or the result,* around which a design or plan is constructed.

> Many people equate purpose with intention. If a person intends to do something, then he or she purposes to do it. So, one way of understanding intentional experience is to see it as goal-directed and purposive. With this perspective, a person's intentional object would be an objective or a perceived outcome or even the result of some process under

consideration. Thus, the term "teleology," which is related to the telos, or the "end or goal toward which a movement is being directed" (Arndt & Gingrich, 1957, p. 819), concerns the study of goal-directed and purposive behavior...the teleological sense of intentional acts is that they are (1) goal directed, (2) focused on purpose and/or outcome, (3) take into consideration function and/or dysfunction, and (4) attempt to be sensitive to the organism-environment parameters that affect behavior. (Brownell, 2010b, pp. 24–26)[1]

Martin, MacKinnon, Johnson, and Rohsenow (2011) pointed to a study that showed people with purpose were more apt to do better in recovery from cocaine addiction. This purpose, this motivation to change, has largely been studied in connection with the beginning of treatment (see the discussion on Motivational Interviewing), but there is evidence that the issue of motivation is important throughout the process of treatment and needs to find attention in order to foster even greater long-term results (Korcha, Polcin, Bond, Lapp, & Galloway, 2011).

When it comes to recovering from addiction, a person has to be invested. As one recovering addict explained it, "You have to have the 'want-to.' " Indeed, common factors research indicates that client factors such as motivation, or the relative discomfort of the client with the status quo, can in many cases account for a majority of the positive outcomes to treatment. These extra-therapeutic factors consist of client and environmental variables and are estimated to account for 40% of variance in outcomes. "These factors include any aspects of the client and his or her environment that, regardless of participation in formal treatment, lead to improvement of the client's presenting concern (e.g., support systems, academic or workplace environments)" (Harris, Aldea, & Kirkley, 2006, p. 615). This indicates that the client and his or her subjective sense of the situation should be the starting place for treatment, and in terms of motivation, the client's relative desire for change becomes an important figure of interest in the ongoing process.

There are many approaches to motivation, but it is helpful to realize that in some cases the desire to achieve something comes from an external source and in other cases it comes from an internal source— external and internal motivation, respectively. In external motivation, a person is pushed and moved by forces outside of him- or herself, forces that are most aligned with a behavioral approach to experience and address regimens of reward or reinforcement and punishment. The internal sense of motivation is more closely aligned with an organismic understanding in which the person is considered to be making choices among alternatives. Internal motivation is concerned with interest, play, curiosity, and exploration and is not dependent on reinforcement for its maintenance. Intrinsic motivation shows itself in an inherent tendency to seek out novelty and challenges, to extend oneself, and to learn. The energy required is intrinsic to the organism (Deci & Ryan, 1985). Ryan and Deci (2000) stated that three innate psychological needs are related to the development of such intrinsic motivation: competence (the sense that one can make things happen), autonomy (the sense of unencumbered agency), and relatedness (the sense of belonging or companionship). They further pointed to research indicating that people who are authentically and internally motivated (as opposed to externally motivated) have more interest, excitement, and confidence, "which in turn is manifest both as enhanced performance, persistence, and creativity" (Ryan & Deci, 2000, p. 68), heightened vitality, self-esteem, and general well-being. Thus, people with demonstrated internal motivation for change will also bring with them the various resources that can make treatment more effective; they use their creativity, they stand on their self-esteem, and they benefit from their persistence.

THE POWER IN A FIGURE OF INTEREST

Both Murray and Maslow created motivational systems around the concept of "need." Before them, Freud and his colleagues posited "drives." However, there was a growing sense in some that "interest" was at least as important; indeed, perhaps it is more important. Gestalt therapists commonly claim that need and/or interest organize the field; that is, need and/or interest bring to foreground what is important to the client. They loom large in the flow of subjective experience, and they cry for attention and resolution. Curiosity may have killed the cat, but it feeds many a human being. The person marshals resources and attempts to meet his or her needs, satisfying his or her interests and indulging his or her curiosities. Yontef (1993) stated that in the normal person

> a configuration is formed which has the qualities of a good gestalt, with the organizing figure being the dominant need ... The individual meets this need by contacting the environment with some sensori-motor behavior. The contact is organized by the figure of interest against the ground of the organism/environment field. (p. 51)

Interest, then, becomes as important as need. Sylvia Crocker (1999) described interested excitement as referring to "the human capacity to take an interest in a situation, and to do so in such a way as to begin to mobilize one's energies and to look for a solution to the emergent problem" (p. 45). She went on to contrast the primary motivator in traditional psychoanalysis (the libido) with that in gestalt therapy, which can be almost anything that stimulates an excited interest. When clients come for help, the gestalt therapist asks questions that increase awareness and sharpen such interest. Such "awareness work must succeed in engaging the person's capacity for interested excitement ..." (Crocker, 1999, p. 54). This is accomplished by engaging the client in a dialogical relationship and exploring the subjective, phenomenal experience of the client. These processes will be explained more fully in subsequent chapters; however, at this point it is important to notice the similarity between the phenomenal exploration of the client's motivation, including his or her prorecovery purposes, and what has become known as "motivational interviewing" (MI).

MOTIVATION RELATED TO TREATMENT FOR ADDICTION

Philosophically, having a reason to do any particular thing tends to motivate one to action; however, according to some, such reasons depend on a primary psychological desire that moves one to find such reasons (Finlay & Schroeder, 2008). By the time this gets seated in front of a therapist in the form of an actual client, there is some mix of emotion and cognition presenting around the goal of stopping what has become an unmanageable behavior. The client desires to escape a negative state and to experience positive emotions (Wagner & Ingersoll, 2008). The client wants to get into recovery, but that's not typically all the client wants.

In the dynamic of addiction, an approach-avoidance cycle develops in which a person approaches the using because of the pleasure it brings, but avoids it also because of the destruction it brings. Thus, an ambivalence develops (Fraser & Solovey, 2007), and in gestalt terminology that means that an impasse has been reached in which the client is stuck between two ends of a polarity. This is also the situation in which the much-favored practice of MI (Miller & Rollnick, 2002) takes place. MI has been widely researched and applied in a number of clinical, research, and outcomes projects, an exhaustive list of which would be a distraction at this point.[2] It is a way of resolving the impasse by emphasizing one side of the ambivalence, and it leads to change; MI has been found to enhance treatment outcomes in a variety of applications by encouraging preparatory speech that focuses on desire, ability, reason or need, and commitment speech in which the client expresses the intent to change (Moyers, Martin, Houck, Christopher, & Tonigan, 2009). Because these arise from the client's own subjective sense of being in the world, and are his or her desires and interests, the dissonance of not pursuing what is in one's best interest (literally) helps to dissolve the ambivalence (and so this is the crux of the theory behind MI).

MI is closely related to the Transtheoretical Model of Change (TTM; Patterson, 2010). The TTM provides a heuristic, a descriptive model of how change takes place across a range of behaviors, whereas MI is a clinical method used to facilitate readiness *to* change:

> While MI does not prescribe specific intervention methods for each stage of change, it is designed to help patients move through such stages of change with a minimum of effort, confrontation, and resistance—more quickly than they might do on their own. (Patterson, 2010, p. 188)

The TTM closely resembles the gestalt cycle of experience (COE), a heuristic model (Gaffney, 2010; Mann, 2010; Woldt & Toman, 2005) derived from the sequence of contacting described in Perls et al. (1951). This resemblance can be seen in Table 3.1.

In a normal COE, there is a fluid and even migration through these various phases, as diffuse sensation gives rise to that particular form of awareness that constitutes the formation of an intentional object—the aboutness of experience—and then the mobilization of energy and resources puts together a plan, the subject moves to action, implementing the plan, and the person learns from the experience by looking back and making an appraisal. People have depicted this process as a bell curve. As Michael Clemmens (2005) has observed, however, the addict's customary COE is more like a spike, because with virtually any stimulation at all, the addict moves directly to his or her drug of choice, bypassing the true aboutness of the experience, let alone any kind of creative review of options with which to deal with it, and goes straight to action. The first thing that comes to mind is to pick up or have a drink, and since this process spins virtually everything else to the periphery of life, every activity becomes associated in some way with using. Thus, the addict has no substantive novelty to reflect on and the familiar process of substance use and abuse creates a quick fix orientation to life that does not evaporate just because the addict enters into sobriety.

TABLE 3-1
TTM and COE Compared

Heuristic		Phases in Process	Description
TTM	1	Pre-contemplation	Person not considering change
COE	1	Sensation	Moved by body process with no distinct figure of interest
CC	1	Fore-contact	Excitement or energy surfaces in response to sensation
TTM	2	Contemplation	Serious evaluation for and against change
COE	2	Awareness	Intentionality, figure formation, the aboutness of experience
TTM	3	Preparation	Planning and commitment secured
COE	3	Mobilization	Considering alternatives and gathering resources
CC	2	Contact	The self moves toward the contact boundary of self and other
TTM	4	Action	Specific behavioral steps are taken
COE	4	Contact	A move to action; plan put into effect
CC	3	Final Contact	Highest sharpness and most intense identification with figure
TTM	5	Maintenance	Work to sustain long term change
COE	5	Assimilation	Making meaning from experience
CC	4	Post-contact	Recession of satisfied figure and entrance into fertile void

TTM, Transtheoretical Model of Change; COE, gestalt cycle of experience; CC, gestalt contact cycle.

Motivational Interviewing

It is against this view of the way interest and bodily sensation forms figures and organizes one's field that we come to the gestalt approach to MI.

Wagner and Ingersoll (2008) claimed that MI could be described as a therapy of emotional emancipation in that MI frees clients from the constraints of paralyzing ambivalence that confuses and customarily keeps them unsure of what to do or how to do it to say nothing about confidence in whether they can change.

> MI is intended to help clients resolve this ambivalence by increasing their sense of desire, need, ability and commitment to change. With ambivalence diminished and commitment to change increased, clients are empowered to seek lives more of their choosing. (p. 191)

Descriptions of MI closely resemble the dialogical approach of gestalt therapy in which the therapist explores the phenomenal aspects of the client's addictive experience, attending to what brings the client in for therapy (engaging the client in change language that is prorecovery in nature). In this dialogical approach, a collaboration forms that is intrinsic to the gestalt understanding of a therapeutic relationship; the power differential is horizontal—one human being to another. The therapist is attempting to evoke a telling of the client's experience by listening and making observations, meeting the client where he or she actually is, and bringing into clearer focus the client's motivation for change, something intrinsic to each individual client, and all this rather than to "transplant or inject it from an external source" (Moyers, 2003, p. 138). As Miller and Rollnick (2002) described it, instead of telling clients that they have a problem, people are asked to simply talk about their own perceptions, their own sense of the situation, and the therapist responds in a largely reflective fashion. Also, instead of telling clients what to do, people are asked what they want to do. Instead of challenging what is perceived to be client resistance, the therapist accepts it as a given and supports it, which is called rolling with the resistance. This process is intended to bring the client to a greater awareness of a greater responsibility for his or her problems with drinking or drugging and to help facilitate a commitment to change. The impetus for change, then, is drawn from the client's world, his or her own motives and goals. It is the client who expresses the desire and the reasons for change (Harris et al., 2006).

The MI therapist uses five principles, arranged in the acrostic that spells "DARES." The therapist Develops discrepancy, Avoids argumentation, Rolls with resistance, Expresses empathy, and Supports self-efficacy (Oetzel, 2010). Developing the discrepancy makes explicit a difference between the status quo and desire for change, and that creates a cognitive dissonance. Avoiding arguments requires the therapist to back away from conflict; it's related to rolling with resistance, in which the therapist uses the momentum of the client by guiding, reflective listening, and affirmations. Expressing empathy means understanding the client's experience. Supporting self-efficacy means the therapist supports the sense of the client that he or she is capable of acting in his or her best interests.

In developing a discrepancy, the MI therapist works with the ambivalence between prorecovery motivation and the motivation to remain using, and this ambivalence can also be seen as a polarity. Polarities in gestalt therapy are simplistic reductions of otherwise complex situations. Instead of seeing gray, the person simplifies the field and reduces it to an either/or perception (MacKewn, 1997). Something is either black or white, but not in between. Thus, with regard to recovery and the treatment it involves, an addict can experience it as alternately good or bad, wanted or not wanted. The client usually identifies with one end of a polarity and alienates the other; however, when someone comes for therapy for addiction, he or she is often responding to an intrinsic wish to identify completely and give oneself wholeheartedly to the recovery end of a polarity but is unable to do so because the other end also calls, and it includes the desire to use one's drug of choice or otherwise avoid making changes to one's lifestyle that seem scary or challenging. The gestalt therapist usually engages the client at both ends and works toward the middle, where the gray and the complexity reside; in MI from a gestalt perspective, the gestalt therapist accentuates the polarity itself, bringing into clearer relief the prorecovery figure of interest at one end and the desire to keep using or drinking at the other. The complexity still develops over time, but at the initial stage of therapy, where MI is usually carried out, the discrepancy in the polarity naturally emerges.

As Miller and Rose (2009) described the process in MI, the model focuses "on responding differentially to client speech, within a generally empathic person-centered style." Special attention is focused on "evoking and strengthening the client's own verbalized motivations for change ..." and counterchange argument, which is known as "sustain talk" or resistance and represents "the other side of the client's ambivalence, to which the counselor" responds empathically (p. 528).

This nonconfrontational approach is done experimentally, not really knowing where the client will take the process, because the process is ultimately uncontrollable and dependent on the strength of the client's intrinsic motivation. The exploration is of the relative phenomenality relating to readiness for change and is focused on the explication of the client's experience.

This is also done dialogically, accepting the client as another subject instead of an object that the therapist needs to "fix" by manipulating or controlling the shape of communication (Brownell, 2010a).[3] Nevertheless, when the gestalt therapist hears the client expressing statements of desire, ability, reasons, and/or need for change (the prorecovery end of the polarity), he or she can know that these lead to commitment, and it is commitment to change that is the greatest predictor of positive outcome in recovery (Miller & Rose, 2009).

A Word About Ambivalence and Impasse

The double interest of the client, this identification with both ends of the polarity while keeping them a polarity, creates the fence-straddling experience of ambivalence that faces the therapist—and as stated already, in gestalt terms it can also be understood as an impasse.

In gestalt therapy, an impasse is usually a point, in the therapeutic process, at which the patient senses a lack of support, either internal or external, and is stuck between moving forward into uncharted territory and resisting change, holding to the status quo—change versus no change (MacKewn, 1997; Yontef, 1993). The impasse is the place where the forces with a person

> are equally distributed between the wish to increase awareness and the felt (but often unconscious) need to block awareness.... It is the place where people's organismic urge to uncover fixed gestalts and premature denials of their real needs is met by the pressure of fixed habits and inertia. (MacKewn, 1997, p. 171)

The gestalt therapist waits on the creative adjustment of the client, not rushing to rescue. The therapist may choose to support the resistance, thus robbing it of fuel, but basically, the therapist "hangs out" with the client in the impasse, maintaining a dialogical relationship, and explores what it's like for both client and therapist to be there. Thus, the addition to customary MI from a gestalt perspective would be the phenomenal exploration of not only the client's desire to change but also the relational support of the client's resistance— supporting the resistance corresponds to "rolling with the resistance" from a purely MI perspective; however, it is also a bit more. The essence of the oft-cited "chair work" in gestalt therapy is the resolving of splits and polarities that are present in the impasse and also present in the ambivalence addressed through MI. Supporting the resistance is the gestalt way of saying that the therapist does not confront or shame the client into prerecovery behavior. The therapist does not push the client into conformity; the therapist waits upon the client to choose recovery, if indeed he or she does. However, the road to that choice in gestalt therapy is abiding the impasse, holding the polarity/ambivalence, and exploring its fullness, while waiting on the shift that can occur when the client, having sat completely with all aspects of the ambivalence, chooses one figure over the other. To integrate the two approaches, the gestalt therapist can listen for prorecovery language, change language, and reflect that.

LISA

"Hi, Lisa."
"Hello."
"Your voice sounds…"

"Down?"

"Yes. What is going on?"

"It's not been more than two weeks and the experiment didn't work."

"What do you mean, it 'didn't work?'"

"I drank. What do you think!?" Her voice had an angry tone to it. "Yes, I'm angry," she said. "I don't like feeling this weak."

"Tell me what happened. Slow it down, and let's take it one frame at a time."

"I went a whole week without drinking. No problems. Felt good. Then, last weekend I got bored, and I don't know what happened. There I was sitting with a vodka tonic in my hand."

"Where did you get the vodka?"

"Well, I had it. You know. Left over."

"And the tonic water?"

"Same."

"I'm wondering how come you didn't get rid of that stuff."

"Well, because it was only an experiment, and so I told myself it was ridiculous to throw away perfectly good vodka and tonic water."

"Because you knew you were going to use them again?"

"Right."

"That makes sense."

"Thank you!"

"To me the experiment worked just fine. There's no success or failure with such things—just an experience to learn from. I'm curious what you have learned from this experiment."

Lisa paused. She was thinking about the idea of an experiment not having a failure attached to it. "No failure?"

"Nope."

"Hm. What did I learn? Well, it seems like part of me is determined to drink no matter what. And the other part, maybe it's not all my desire to not drink, but for whatever reason I tell myself that I'm not going to drink, but then I do...and then it gets all crazy."

"Well," said the therapist, "there does seem to be a discrepancy between telling yourself you're not going to drink and the fact that you do drink. What are some reasons why you might want to stop your drinking, or at least cut down on the amount you drink?"

"I don't like feeling weak and out of control...Uh, the money. I could sure save a bit more money if I weren't pouring it down my throat every day."

"What about your health and your ability to function?"

"Yeah. Sure. There's that. It scares me to think that I could be 'out there' so blitzed that I can't remember what I've been doing, and I could get into trouble."

"You up for another kind of experiment, one we can do right here and now?"

"What is it?"

Well, let's imagine there are two Lisa's. One wants to continue to drink and the other wants to quit drinking. The quit-drinking Lisa is sitting over on that couch, and the keep-drinking Lisa is sitting at the other end of the couch you're on right now. Can you sort of see them?"

"Yeah."

"Okay, move down a bit on your couch and be the 'keep-drinking Lisa.' Tell the 'quit-drinking Lisa' why you want to keep drinking."

She scootched over, looked back across the room to where she imagined the "quit-drinking Lisa" was sitting and said, "I don't want to quit. I like the buzz. I like forgetting how nervous I feel around people in crowds. I like feeling happy. I like the 'me' I am on alcohol."

"Okay," said the therapist, "Now move over to that couch, be the 'quit-drinking Lisa' and talk back to the 'keep-drinking Lisa.' Tell her why you want to quit drinking."

She did and said, "It's not like it used to be, and you are not stopping where you used to stop. I don't like what it feels like to get so blitzed I can't recall what was I was doing, to feel so sick, to spend all that money, to risk losing my job, and to feel myself running myself down. It's not healthy, and I know it. I know it inside; nobody has to tell me, and I feel guilty and weak and pathetic when I don't do those things that I know are good for me, even while I'm doing things that I know are bad for me. I thought it wasn't as bad as it is."

The therapist invited Lisa to move back to where she was before the experiment. He said, "Now look this way and that, at both Lisas. They are both you, aren't they?"

"Yes," she said. "Both me."

"What's that like? To sit with them both like that?"

"Nuts. Even if I wanted to stop drinking, even if I told myself that I can't afford to drink, I don't know if I *can* stop drinking."

"Hm. What I know is the person I'm sitting with right now just did a challenging experiment that not everyone can do. You have a record of achievement in life. I think it's ultimately up to you, but my guess is that you can do it. If you could do it, how much would you like to do it? Figure it this way, if "1" is not at all and "10 is absolutely, then where are you with wanting to quit drinking?"

"I'm about... well, I'm about a 6."

"Ah, I notice that when you were the 'quit-drinking Lisa' you did not mention wanting to quit so that you could keep your job. Why didn't you mention that?"

"They are making me come here. I thought you wanted me to say the reasons I want to quit. If I quit to keep my job, it's like quitting because they want me to quit."

"Ah. That feels bad?"

"Right! I don't want to do anything just because somebody else tells me to do it."

"So, there are reasons why you want to quit and they don't have anything to do with what other people want you to do. Is that right?"

"Yes. I want to quit, but I just don't know if I can quit, because I didn't do so hot for the last two weeks, and there's still a part of me that wants to drink."

"Fair enough. That gives us something to talk about next time, if you want."

CONCLUSION

People have to want to change. Their motivation to change is one of the factors most relevant to positive outcomes, not just in matters of addiction, but across the board in all matters relating to psychotherapy outcomes. The most potent kind of motivation is intrinsic motivation, that which arises from within a person according to his or her own figures of interest. Gestalt therapy's conception of polarities, and specifically the polarity that exists in a person between desire for the status quo and desire for change, provides for an easy assimilation of the practice of MI. When assimilated into the normal flow of gestalt process, all the research on MI becomes available to the gestalt practitioner working with addicted individuals. That at once lends empirical support for gestalt practice and enlarges the gestalt process itself. This exceeds mere integration or eclecticism, because gestalt therapy has a long history of working with the ambivalence in polarities, and the stuck point of the impasse, it actually has something to contribute to those who use MI in their practices originating from other clinical perspectives. Although MI is most often conceived of as a stand-alone technique to be used in conjunction with some established treatment regimen, when understood as being intrinsic to gestalt process, it is possible to use MI at various stages in the continuing work and to actually see MI as having a basic clinical model to which it naturally belongs. Part II of the book summarizes the core tenets of that approach, but a more complete development of them can be found in this author's book, *Gestalt Therapy: A Guide to Contemporary Practice* (2010a).

NOTES

1. The phenomenological sense of intentionality will be explained in Chapter 4.
2. A search at the American Psychological Association's (APA) PycInfo database on June 20, 2011, provided 1,448 results.
3. Thus, a gestalt therapist does not treat the client as an object, a thing, in what Buber would call an I–It form of relationship, but meets the client as a transcendent "other" who defies thematization, totalization, and utilization, and who is another subject—a Thou.

REFERENCES

Arndt, W. F., & Gingrich, F. W. (1957). *A Greek-English lexicon of the New Testament and other early Christian literature.* Chicago, IL: The University of Chicago Press.

Brownell, P. (2010a). *Gestalt therapy: A guide to contemporary practice.* New York: Springer Publishing.

Brownell, P. (2010b). Intentional spirituality. In J. Ellens (Ed.), *The healing power of spirituality: How faith helps humans thrive* (Vol. 1 personal spirituality, pp. 24–26). Santa Barbara, Denver, CO: Praeger/ABC-CLIO.

Clemmens, M. (2005). *Getting beyond sobriety: Clinical approaches to long-term recovery.* Cambridge, MA: GestaltPress.

Conroy, D., Elliot, A., & Thrash, T. (2009). Achievement motivation. In M. Leary, & R. Hoyle (Eds.), *Handbook of individual differences in social behavior* (pp. 382–399). New York: Guilford Press.

Crocker, S. (1999). *A well-lived life: Essays in gestalt therapy.* Cambridge, MA: GIC Press.

Cunningham, C., Wakefield, J., & Ward, R. (1975). An empirical comparison of Maslow's and Murray's needs systems. *Journal of Personality Assessment, 39*(6), 594–596.

Deci, E., & Ryan, R. (1985). *Intrinsic motivation and self-determination in human behavior.* New York: Plenum Press.

Finlay, S., & Schroeder, M. (2008). Reasons for action: Internal vs external. In E. N. Zalta (Ed.), *The Stanford Encyclopedia of Philosophy.* Retrieved June 20, 2011, from http://plato.stanford.edu/entries/reasons-internal-external

Fraser, J., & Solovey, A. (2007). Substance abuse and dependency. In J. Fraser, & A. Solovey (Eds.), *Second-order change in psychotherapy: The golden thread that unifies effective treatments* (pp. 223–244). Washington, DC: American Psychological Association.

Gaffney, S. (2010). The cycle of experience recycled: Then, now...next? *Gestalt Review, 13*(1), 7–23.

Harris, R., Jr., Aldea, M., & Kirkley, D. (2006). A motivational interviewing and common factors approach to change in working with alcohol use and abuse in college students. *Professional Psychology: Research and Practice, 37*(6), 614–621.

Korcha, R. A., Polcin, D. L., Bond, J. C., Lapp, W. M., & Galloway, G. (2011). Substance use and motivation: A longitudinal perspective. *The American Journal of Drug and Alcohol Abuse, 37*(1), 48–53.

Lewin, K. (1940). Review of explorations in personality. *The Journal of Abnormal and Social Psychology, 35*(2), 283–285.

MacKewn, J. (1997). *Developing gestalt counselling.* London, England: SAGE.

Mann, D. (2010). *Gestalt therapy: 100 key points and techniques.* New York: Routledge.

Martin, R., MacKinnon, S., Johnson, J., & Rohsenow, D. (2011). Purpose in life predicts treatment outcome among adult cocaine abusers in treatment. *Journal of Substance Abuse Treatment, 40*(2), 183–188.

Maslow, A. (1954/1987). *Motivation and personality* (3rd ed.). New York: Harper & Row.

Miller, W., & Rollnick, S. (2002). *Motivational interviewing: Preparing people for change.* New York: Guilford Press.

Miller, W., & Rose, G. (2009). Toward a theory of motivational interviewing. *American Psychologist, 64*(6), 527–537.

Moyers, T. (2003). Motivational interviewing. In J. Sorensen, R. Rawson, J. Guydish, & J. Zweben (Eds.), *Drug abuse treatment through collaboration: Practice and research partnerships that work* (pp. 139–150). Washington, DC: American Psychological Association.

Moyers, T., Martin, T., Houck, J., Christopher, P., & Tonigan, J. (2009). From in-session behaviors to drinking outcomes: A causal chain for motivational interviewing. *Journal of Consulting and Clinical Psychology, 77*(6), 1113–1124.

Murray, H. (1938). *Explorations of personality.* Oxford, England: Oxford University Press.

Oetzel, K. (2010). *Motivational interviewing.* Training lecture. Retrieved June 10, 2011, from http://www.youtube.com/watch?v=CozBbGyPK_k&NR=1

Patterson, D. (2010). Motivational interviewing. In D. Patterson (Ed.), *Clinical hypnosis for pain control* (pp. 185–209). Washington, DC: American Psychological Association.

Perls, F., Hefferline, R., & Goodman, P. (1951). *Gestalt therapy: Excitement and growth in the human personality.* London, England: Souvenir Press.

Ryan, R., & Deci, L. (2000). Self-determination theory and facilitation of intrinsic motivation, social development, and well-being. *American Psychologist, 55*(1), 68–78.

Yontef, G. (1993) *Awareness, Dialogue, and Process.* Highland, NY: Gestalt Journal Press.

Wagner, C., & Ingersoll, K. (2008). Beyond cognition: Broadening the base of motivational interviewing. *Journal of Psychotherapy Integration, 18*(2), 191–206.

Woldt, A., & Toman, S. (2005). *Gestalt therapy history, theory, and practice.* Thousand Oaks, CA: SAGE.

II

An Approach to Treatment

4

The Nature of Individual Experience

This chapter explores the gestalt therapy tenet of individual experience, including the phenomenological method employed by gestalt therapists to follow an individual's experience. There are many aspects to all this, but a starting point is in the way a therapist can follow a client's unfolding experience and use descriptions of it that heighten the awareness of the client with regard to what he or she is doing and how he or she is doing it.

There is a flow of life, a rhythm and a current to its process. At any moment in time we are immersed in its river. Where I grew up, people rent rafts and drift down the American River, which flows out of Folsom Reservoir, through the Nimbus Dam, and then downstream toward Sacramento in the wide and flat central valley of California. There are no thrilling white water stretches in that place. You just get in at one point and drift to another. Along the way, you talk with the other people in your raft, and from time to time something along the way catches your attention. You bring food. You bring drink. It is a lazy way to spend some time in the sun. It is relaxing and exciting all at the same time, and that's because people get "into" it.

Being thoroughly invested in what one is doing means identifying with one's state, which implies knowing what one's actual experience or situation is, and because nothing remains static, this also means identifying with the flow of one's states, trusting in the current of life (Yontef, 1993). As a figure of interest emerges from the situational background, the person identifies with that figure and becomes so invested, so immersed, that the background drops away and out of awareness (Perls, Hefferline, & Goodman, 1951) even though it is always there to offer context for the interpretation of experience.

This subjective sense of being in the world is an embodied experience. How could it be anything but that? Our bodies are our instruments for contacting the world, but they are more than our instruments; they are us. A person might say, "I hurt my arm," which sounds like the arm is something outside of the person him- or herself, but if one person touches another's arm, that person is just as apt to hear, "You touched my arm" or "You touched me." They are interchangeable.

Kepner (2001) asserted that an integrated and holistic approach to psychotherapy was one in which people had a sufficient degree of body awareness together with an adequate sense of the relationship between oneself and one's current issues, coupled with a trust that both body and psychological processes were related to those issues—awareness of body, awareness of issues, and trust that these are related.

It is through the body, even from the beginning of one's life, that one forms patterns of contacting with one's environment, and experiences patterns of response in return.

> Beginning in the womb and emerging throughout the first years of life, developmental movement patterns facilitate the earliest formation of self-perception and other perception, self-knowing and discovery of the other. In this way, developmental movements underlie the progressive articulation of me and not me. (Frank, 2001, p. 41)

The realization that what the body is doing both represents the functioning of the self and the development of self-experience leads to ways in which gestalt therapists attempt to work with a whole person in psychotherapy. Gestalt therapists attend to the body, not in the sense of interpreting body nonverbals as if with a manual that identifies taxonomies of movements and gestures and tells the therapist "this" means "that" and "that" means "this." Rather, it's the whole person in movement. It's the whole person shining through the body, and it's the body process that reveals one and calls to the other. So, gestalt therapists attend to the way a person carries the body—the body at work and the body at rest, the body walking, standing, sitting, speaking, crying, hiding, asserting, protecting, and playing. These things provide the gestalt therapist with handles necessary to practice a phenomenological method.

A PHENOMENOLOGICAL APPROACH

In their recent book, *Mindfulness-Based Relapse Prevention for Addictive Behaviors: A Clinician's Guide*, Bowen, Chawla, and Marlatt (2011) described what is essentially a phenomenological process. They assert that in a mindfulness approach, the intention is to keep centered on present experience, relating that experience to relapse and other recovery-related issues and lifestyle factors, but all the while keeping the inquiry focused on direct experience. This reflects the central purpose of such mindful practices, which is to notice what actually arises in each moment rather than to get deflected into interpretations and stories of events that happened at another time and place. This process

> requires facilitators to continually redirect each interaction to a description of the immediate experience in the present moment (i.e., sensations in the body, thoughts, or emotions) versus the interpretation, analysis, or story about the experience. (Bowen, Chawla, & Marlatt, 2011, p. 6)

Ernesto Spinelli (2005) described such a phenomenological method by asserting that it comprised several steps: the rule of epoché, the rule of description, and the rule of horizontalization. In the rule of epoché, one sets aside initial biases and commitments, suspending assumptions in order to focus on the primary manifestation of immediate experience. In the rule of description, one describes rather than explains. As Spinelli depicts it, the rule of description "urges us to remain initially focused on our immediate and concrete impressions and to maintain a level of analysis with regard to these experiences which takes description rather than theoretical explanation or speculation as its point of focus" (pp. 20–21). The rule of horizontalization moves one to "avoid placing any initial hierarchies of significance or importance upon the items of our descriptions, and instead to treat each initially as having equal value or significance" (p. 21).

In gestalt therapy, this boils down to three steps: observe, bracket, and describe. First, one trains him- or herself to systematically and carefully observe what is happening between therapist and client as the therapeutic process unfolds. Largely this means focusing on what the client is doing and saying, and how he or she is doing that, but everything that takes place between them is a co-constructed reality (see later section). Second, one brackets whatever countertransference or model-making thoughts occur to the therapist. Third, one simply speaks forth, describes what one is observing, and then stops to wait for the client's response. It is a descriptive following of the manifestations of the client's phenomenality—what the client experiences in the presence of the therapist.

The phenomenological process in mindfulness meditation and the phenomenological process in gestalt therapy are consilient; that is, there is a "jumping together" of knowledge in which what is true in one domain is also true in another. The gestalt therapy emphasis on current subjective experience is convergent with mindfulness and acceptance therapy. In explicating how gestalt therapy process and mindfulness meditation overlap one another, Eva Gold and Steve Zahm (2011) list various, convergent features between them:

1. Phenomenological method—attending to actual sensory data, suspending preconceived ideas
2. Field—everything is part of an interconnected field and nothing exists in isolation
3. How change occurs—being with "what is" allows the natural flow of experience, which is always changing
4. Importance of the present moment—this is the only place awareness can occur, and therefore, it is the ground for growth and insight
5. Focus on bodily experience—the importance of the "felt sense" vs. conceptualizing or talking about
6. Therapist stance—being fully present, accepting what is, seeing the other as precious, no hierarchy
7. Holistic—no aspect of human functioning or experience is left out, and all are seen as interconnected (Gold & Zahm, 2011)

These are bullet points in a process that points the therapist to the way in which the client experiences him- or herself living, moving, and having being in the world. Whatever it is like to be the client at any particular time, especially at the time he or she is sitting with the therapist, is manifest in the way the client presents. It is the presence of the client that provides a phenomenon for the therapist. It calls to the therapist, and the therapist experiences this call in his or her response to the client. "We hear the call only in the answer, in a voice that has been altered by it . . ." (Chrétien, 2004, p. 27). The call of the client cannot be known except in the response of the therapist. This is the profound impact of the client as another person, an "other" who transcends our usual ways of knowing, interpreting, and organizing the inputs we receive from the environment. The client is not simply our construction of meaning; we cannot make him or her up in familiar words and models that we use to refer to the world as we know it. The client is unique and transcendent (Levinas, 1999). To thematize the client, giving him or her labels and categorizing his or her behaviors, is to do what Emmanuel Levinas calls "a violence" to the client (Smith, 2002).

The phenomenological method referred to in the preceding was created by Edmund Husserl as a philosophical process with a philosophical purpose to accomplish his philosophical project. That project was to create a tool by which scientists might get at things in the

world themselves. The philosophy of intentionality and phenomenological perception is beyond the scope of this book. It is also somewhat beyond the scope of a method that has since been adapted for
psychological purposes. In simple language, we are interested in the
way the client experiences being in the world, observing and creating
"concrete descriptions of experienced events from the perspective of
everyday life by participants ..." (Giorgi & Giorgi, 2003, p. 251). We are
therapists working with tangible people and not philosophers working with abstract ideas. Although philosophy is helpful to train one's
thinking, we operate in the natural attitude, taking at face value what
we see and what we hear while in the presence of the client. We are
not looking for the essence of the client somewhere below his or her
obvious presentation. We may be observing patterns out of the client's
awareness, but this is quite different from reducing the natural attitude to a transcendental attitude (Luft, 1998). We are looking for what
it is like to be the client in the midst of his or her circumstances, how
he or she senses being in the situation; in fact, we are looking for how
the client finds him- or herself there (Gendlin, 1978–1979). This is an
examination, a careful and qualitative investigation of the client's subjective experience. In gestalt therapy, therefore, one uses a modified
phenomenological method (Burley & Bloom, 2008). In moving beyond
and refining Husserl's philosophical approach, Don Ihde (1977) proposed three steps: (1) attend to phenomena as they show themselves,
(2) describe (don't explain) phenomena, and (3) horizontalize all phenomena initially.

What clinical purpose might it serve to simply follow the phenomenality of the client? What good is it to make the client more aware
of the current moment in which he or she is doing this or that in any
given manner? Doesn't the gestalt therapist make clinical judgments
about what is going on with the client? Doesn't it matter what the cause
of the disorder might be?

Here-and-Now Phenomenality and Paradoxical Change

Gestalt therapy's theory of change is paradoxical. This should not
be confused with the paradoxical interventions of therapists such
as Jay Haley, in which the therapist sought to achieve change by
prescribing the problem (Haley & Greenberg, 2010). As will be
seen, that would be directly antithetical to the approach of a gestalt
therapist.

Naturally, there are many aspects to change; however, Arnold Beisser
(1970) described what became a standard assertion of how change occurs

in gestalt therapy, saying that people change by actualizing who they are in the current moment. In his own words, "Change occurs when one becomes what he is, not when he tries to become what he is not" (p. 77). Getting to something distant only starts with something present. "Bringing into awareness is fundamental for change... Awareness, by definition, changes us" (Melnick, Nevis, & Shub, 2005). Therefore, to focus on the current moment and to attend to a client's subjective experience *there* (the here and now) is a powerful impetus for change (Clegg, 2010; Truscott, 2010). "To heal a suffering one must experience it to the full" (Beisser, 1970, p. 78).

To change, we must inhabit our experience, our consciousness of self. What is it like to do that? It is always a work in progress with people taking up more or less residence at any given time. Gallagher and Zahavi (2008) believed that it made sense to speak of self-consciousness whenever they consciously perceived something in their environment, such as a rock, a bed, a book case, or a pet, because

> to consciously perceive something is not simply to be conscious of the perceptual object, but also to be acquainted with the experience of the object. In its most primitive and fundamental form, self-consciousness is simply a question of ongoing first-personal manifestation of experiential life. (p. 49)

This is not the kind of self-consciousness in which one feels socially awkward or conspicuous. This is being aware of being situated, of being in a place in time with others. The tracking of the client's phenomenality produces immediate experience of the self that is linked to the client's presenting addiction issues and dynamics, but, as was seen with the similarity to motivational interviewing, these things arise from the client as the client becomes increasingly aware of what he or she is doing and how he or she is doing it. This awareness emerges from the observing and describing activities of the therapist.

What is the therapist observing when such observing takes place? It is a current experience of the whole person. It is important to understand that the client may be talking about something that has happened last week or yesterday, that might happen tomorrow, or that took place when he or she was a child. The therapist is not interested in finding out the facts of the story the client is telling.[1] The therapist follows the experience of the telling. The story is the client's basket, and it carries feelings and the meanings the client has made from experience. The parts of the story form a structure that organizes the experience into a meaningful and coherent whole, and it is a meaning that is significant to the client. This requires a hermeneutic phenomenological method, one that unpacks the basket in coordination with the client's telling or reliving of the story.

This is not accomplished by interpreting the client from outside the current moment, from outside the current experience of the client who is caught up in the telling,[2] and it is the client who needs to connect the dots and interpret his or her own story. In the Perls et al. (1951) text, they refer to a "gestalt analysis" of the situation of the client, and by that they mean a clear, telling description of as many elements in the current situation as possible, allowing the parts to illuminate the whole—not in an additive fashion in which parts add up to a whole, but in a suggestive fashion. As more and more description and exploration of the parts of the client's current experience are provided, the "action potential" of a shift of awareness comes closer and closer until it breaks through, and the "synapse" of awareness is achieved in which the client makes a connection of some kind among elements of his or her life. The significance in such cases belongs to the client, and it is grounded in the often very energetic experience of the client's interaction with the therapist. By attending to the current moment, "The gestalt therapist rejects the role of 'changer,' for his strategy is to encourage, even insist, that the patient be where and what he is" (Crocker, 1999, p. 227).

> Change then occurs spontaneously and without effort through awareness of what and how we are thinking, feeling, and doing—through awareness of the field of our present moment. The ensuing process leads to changes in the entire field that is the client's existence. (Truscott, 2010, p. 88)

The paradoxical approach to change, largely in the form of acceptance and commitment therapy,[3] has seen significant growth in interest, with attending research showing its effectiveness. In the process, this interest and focus increases the appreciation of the gestalt therapy construct, which is so central to its approach—the paradoxical nature of acceptance and personal change (Hernández-López, Luciano, Bricker, Rales-Nieto, & Montesinos, 2009; Twohig et al., 2010; Williams & Lynn, 2010).

Also in this regard (and as a brief aside), the affinity between the third wave in cognitive–behavioral therapy and some of the long-standing concepts in gestalt therapy is striking. For instance, Federici, Rowa, and Antony (2010) noted that acceptance and mindfulness-based therapies are based on two essential principles: (1) psychological distress is maintained by effort to avoid or suppress emotional experience and (2) people cannot change or respond effectively to what they do not perceive, acknowledge, or accept. Mindfulness and acceptance therapies hope to

> decrease experiential avoidance while fostering an attitude of openness, curiosity, and acceptance of one's internal world...In other words, the ability to nonjudgmentally view experience without having to act on it tends to decrease distress while enhancing one's awareness and understanding of one's thoughts, emotions, and sensations. (Federici, Rowa, & Antony, 2010, p. 22)

GILBERT AND MELISSA

The room became a triangle when Gilbert and Melissa entered. He sat on one couch. Melissa sat on the other. The therapist sat across the room, but between them. It was a silent triangle. Melissa and Gilbert did not look at one another. Gilbert's countenance seemed irritated, and Melissa resembled a trapped and exhausted animal. Her eyes gave away her pain and desperation. Although there was no sound in the room, the tension was screaming.

> The therapist said, "I notice you're sitting on different couches."
> Melissa had crossed her legs and the one on top started moving in a rapid fashion.
> The therapist said, "You're kicking?"
> "Damn straight I'm kicking! I'd like to kick him." She was talking to the therapist, still not looking at Gilbert. "He's going away to rehab tomorrow, so he takes the opportunity to go on a binge as one last hurrah? Give me a break!"
> "Gil, you're pretty quiet over there."
> "What is there to say," said Gilbert. When he said that, he diverted his eyes from the therapist, shifted to a lower tone at the end of his sentence, and slumped his shoulders.
> "You're not looking at me."
> "Right." He continued to look away.
> The therapist asked him, "What is it like for you right now?"
> Gilbert had planted his elbow on one arm of the couch, and his chin and mouth were cupped in his hand. From that position he gazed at the floor and spoke in a muffled fashion, his words filtered through his fingers. "Pretty shitty. I'd just like to disappear."
> Melissa picked up on his tone, and she shifted stance. She said, "Well, honey, you just need to get into that rehab program ..."

The therapist spoke again to Gilbert, and he said, "You'd like to disappear. What thoughts and feelings are you having that go along with that?"

Gilbert's eyes started to glisten. His eyelids relaxed. Tears formed.

The therapist noticed all that, and he said, "Gil, can you let that keep coming, and can you give those tears a voice? What are they saying?"

"They're saying 'What a loser. What a liar! You'll never get over this. It's gunna take you all the way down.'" Now the tears were rolling down his face.

"Keep breathing. What else are you feeling?"

Gil looked at the therapist, and he said, "I'm feeling hopeless and I'm thinking she's gunna leave me."

Melissa started to speak. She wanted to reassure him and tell him that she wasn't going anywhere, but the therapist stopped her.

"Where in your body do you feel this hopelessness?" he asked Gil. "Can you touch it?"

Gil put his hand on his head and said, "I'm thinking 'who would stick around a loser like me?'"

The therapist said, "Does that seem like an accusation?"

"Yes. It feels like the whole universe is accusing me, like the verdict in a court."

"Is the verdict in? Or is the jury still out? What feelings come up for you as you sense this accusation?"

"I'm scared."

"Can you say that again?"

"I'm scared. I'm afraid Melissa is going to leave me."

"Can you say it again, only this time can you look at Melissa and say it to her?"

Gil took his hand off his mouth, shifted his weight on the couch, turned toward Melissa, looked her in the eye and said, "I'm scared you're going to leave me."

Melissa gushed. She got up and walked over to where Gil was on the other couch, sat down next to him, put her arms around him, caressed his head, and said, "I'm not going to leave you. I'll never leave you."

The therapist said, "You just said that you would never leave him?"

"Yes," she said. She seemed slightly irritated to be distracted from her caressing.

The therapist said, "Just a few minutes ago you were angry and him, and I'm wondering where that feeling went."

"Well, he needs me."

"So, you'd be willing to stay with him even if he goes on a binge?"

"Yes." She said that cautiously, sensing that the therapist was going somewhere with it.

"Just a few minutes ago you seemed disgusted with him, but I notice you softened your attitude when he started to cry."

"Yes."

"Would you be willing to stay with him as long as he cried every time he went on a binge? What if he dropped out of rehab, came back and told you that he was done with recovery, and he intended to keep drinking? Would that be okay?"

She took her hands and arms away from Gil and sat back in the couch. "No," she said.

The therapist said, "I notice your lips are tight and there is tension around your eyes."

Melissa said, "Right. I'm not willing to live like that."

"Meaning that you would leave him if he avoided recovery?"

She paused and then said, "I suppose."

"Is that your resolve right now? On a scale of 1 to 10, with 1 being *I will never leave him if he drinks* to 10 being *I'll leave him the instant he takes another drink*, where are you right this minute?"

"I'm a 7."

The therapist turned to Gilbert, and he said, "She's a 7, man. How's that feel?"

"Scary. But better than a 10. And better than she's out the door right now."

"Ah. You were afraid she was going to leave you right now? Did you think you'd blown it so badly everything was over and all was lost?"

"Yes."

"Sounds like there is a little breathing room, but that it's time to get serious."

"I thought I was serious before."

"Uh-huh. Well, in terms of being committed to change, on a 10-point scale, if you were a 5 before, where are you right now?"

"I'm all in."

"What's that?"

"I'm at an 8 or a 9."

Melissa chuckled. "You are 'all in,' but that's just an 8 or a 9?"

"Well, I don't know if I can do it."

The therapist said, "Let me ask you another one. Right this minute, on a 10-point scale measuring confidence in your ability to change, with 1 being *none at all* and 10 being *totally*, where are you?"

"I'm at a 4."

"What would it take you to be a little more confident in your ability to change?"

"I guess if I had a bit more sober time under my belt...if I'd resisted the temptation to drink."

"Right now as we sit here together, do you think it's possible that you
will get some more sober time under your belt?"

"Well, I suppose I'm going to get some when I go away to rehab."

Melissa sat up and forward again on the couch next to Gil, and she told
him, "You *are* going to get some, because damn it all, you're going
away tomorrow!"

NOTES

1. It is not that facts are totally irrelevant, as accurate information that clients
often minimize or deny to themselves and others are very relevant, but in
terms of this part of therapy—this aspect of the gestalt approach to working with clients—what is most relevant is how the client views what he or
she is saying, what it means to him or her, and how they experience thinking about it.
2. Gestalt therapy is a unified approach, so what I am saying at this point
washes over into other elements of the praxis. The therapist is with the
client in a co-created field, and the therapist is engaged with the client in a
dialogical relationship, and their shared experience is ultimately not determined; the process is experimental at its base and may be filled with various experiments. These things will be dealt with in subsequent chapters.
3. The reader should understand that it is the fundamental assumption
behind the specific therapeutic strategies that are so similar; adaptation,
acceptance, and commitment therapy (ACT) employs various goal-directed
techniques that exceed the gestalt approach.

REFERENCES

Beisser, A. (1970). The paradoxical theory of change. In J. Fagan & E. Shepherd
(Eds.), *Gestalt therapy now: Theory, techniques, applications* (pp. 77–80). Palo
Alto, CA: Science and Behavior Books.

Bowen, S., Chawla, N., & Marlatt, G. (2011). *Mindfulness-based relapse prevention
for addictive behaviors: A clinician's guide.* New York: Guilford Press.

Burley, T., & Bloom, D. (2008). Phenomenological method. In P. Brownell (Ed.),
Handbook for theory, research, and practice in gestalt therapy (pp. 151–183).
Newcastle, England: Cambridge Scholars Publishing.

Chrétien, J-L. (2004). *The call and the response.* New York: Fordham University
Press.

Clegg, K. (2010). Some gestalt contributions to psychiatry. *Journal of Psychiatric
Practice, 16*(4), 250–252.

Crocker, S. (1999). *A well-live life: Essays in gestalt therapy.* Cambridge, MA:
Gestalt Institute of Cleveland Press.

Federici, A., Rowa, J., & Antony, M. (2010). Adjusting treatment for partial- or non-response to contemporary cognitive–behavioral therapy. In D. McKay, J. Abramowitz, & S. Taylor (Eds.), *Cognitive–behavioral therapy for refractory cases: Turning failure into success* (pp. 11–37). Washington, DC: American Psychological Association.

Frank, R. (2001). *Body of awareness: A somatic and developmental approach to psychotherapy.* Cambridge, MA: GestaltPress.

Gallagher, S., & Zahavi, D. (2008). *The phenomenological mind: An introduction to philosophy of mind and cognitive science.* New York: Routledge.

Gendlin, E. (1978–1979). Befindlichkeit: Heidegger and the philosophy of psychology. *Review of Existential Psychology & Psychiatry: Heidegger and Psychology, 16*(1,2,3). Retrieved June 15, 2011, from http://www.focusing.org/gendlin_befindlichkeit.html

Giorgi, A., & Giorgi, B. (2003). The descriptive phenomenological psychological method. In P. Camic, J. Rhodes, & L. Yardley (Eds.), *Qualitative research in psychology: Expanding perspectives in methodology and design* (pp. 243–274). Washington, DC: American Psychological Association.

Gold, E., & Zahm, S. (2011). Gestalt therapy training integrating Buddhist psychology and mindfulness meditation. In D. Bloom & P. Brownell (Eds.), *Continuity and change: Gestalt therapy now, the 10th biennial conference of the Association for the Advancement of Gestalt Therapy.* Newcastle, England: Cambridge Scholars Publishing.

Haley, J., & Greenberg, L. (2010). How to be a marriage therapist without knowing practically anything. In J. Haley, M. Richport-Haley, & J. Carlson (Eds.), *Jay Haley revisited* (pp. 189–209). New York: Routledge.

Hernández-López, M., Luciano, M., Bricker, J., Rales-Nieto, J., & Montesinos, F. (2009). Acceptance and commitment therapy for smoking cessation: A preliminary study of its effectiveness in comparison with cognitive behavioral therapy. *Psychology of Addictive Behaviors, 23*(4), 723–730.

Ihde, D. (1977). *Experimental phenomenology: An introduction.* New York: G.P. Putnam Sons.

Kepner, J. (2001). *Body process: A gestalt approach to working with the body in psychotherapy.* Cambridge, MA: GestaltPress.

Levinas, E. (1999). *Alterity and transcendence.* New York: Columbia University Press.

Luft, S. (1998). Husserl's phenomenological discovery of the natural attitude. *Continental Philosophy Review, 31,* 153–170.

Melnick, J., Nevis, S., & Shub, N. (2005). Gestalt therapy methodology. In A. Woldt & S. Toman (Eds.), *Gestalt therapy history, theory, and practice* (pp. 101–115). London, England: Sage.

Perls, F., Hefferline, R., & Goodman, P. (1951). *Gestalt therapy: Excitement and growth in the human personality.* London, England: Souvenir Press.

Smith, J. K. A. (2002). *Speech and theology: Language and the logica of incarnation.* New York: Routledge.

Spinelli, E. (2005). *The interpreted world: An introduction to phenomenological psychology.* London, England: Sage.

Truscott, D. (2010). Gestalt. In D. Truscott (Ed.), *Becoming an effective psycho-therapist: Adopting a theory of psychotherapy that's right for you and your client* (pp. 83–96). Washington, DC: American Psychological Association.

Twohig, M., Hayes, S., Plumb, J., Pruitt, L., Collins, A., Hazlett-Stevens, H., & Woidneck, M. (2010). A randomized clinical trial of acceptance and com-mitment therapy versus progressive relaxation training for obsessive–compulsive disorder. *Journal of Consulting and Clinical Psychology, 78*(5), 705–716.

Williams, J., & Lynn, S. (2010). Acceptance: An historical and conceptual review. *Imagination, Cognition, and Personality, 30*(1), 5–56.

Yontef, G. (1993) Awareness, dialogue & process. Highland, NY: Gestalt Journal Press.

5

The Importance of Relationships

*This chapter explores the gestalt therapy tenet of dialogue
in which two persons, each with a subjective sense
and experience, meet in relationship. It describes how
nonindependence makes for a mutually constructed experience
and explains the importance of relationship in the context of
psychotherapy and recovery work.*

RELATIONSHIP CRITICAL TO POSITIVE OUTCOME

It is no surprise that a quality therapeutic relationship is critical to
positive outcomes in psychotherapy (Norcross & Wampold, 2011). This
is true for addiction work as well. A sound therapeutic relationship is
five to ten times more crucial to positive outcomes in addiction work
than the particular therapeutic approach used (Mee-Lee, McLellan, &
Miller, 2010). Such an alliance represents an emergent quality charac-
teristic of partnership and mutual collaboration between therapist and
client that

> is not the outcome of a particular or typical intervention. Its develop-
> ment can take different forms and may be achieved quickly or nurtured
> over a longer period of time depending on the kind of therapy and the
> stage of treatment. (Horvath, Del Re, Flückiger, & Symonds, 2011, p. 11)

Norcross and Lambert (2011) defined the therapeutic relationship as
"... the feelings and attitudes that therapist and client have toward
one another, and the manner in which these are expressed" (p. 5). This
is a genuine relationship in which the therapist models the congru-
ence between what he or she presents to others and what the therapist

knows of him- or herself inside; the therapist is freely him- or herself and able to communicate what his or her experience of the client is like to the client (Kolden, Klein, Wang, & Austin, 2011).

Warmth, empathy, acceptance, and support for taking a risk in the therapeutic process loom large. There is also evidence that a focus on objectives and goals contributes to the working alliance between therapist and client, especially when working with men, who are encouraged by the therapist dealing with relevant issues (Bedi & Richards, 2011; Webb et al., 2011). Although creating a connection with the client is crucial during early phases of therapy (to keep the client from early termination), there is also evidence that a good working alliance during sessions 3 through 9 provides about four times the positive outcomes than during sessions 1 to 3 (Crits-Christoph, Gibbons, Hamilton, Ring-Kurtz, & Gallop, 2011).

What takes place in session often leads to the client continuing to process the experience outside of session. Such intersession processes describe the degree to which clients think about their therapy between sessions and how they chew on and continue to work through what has taken place with the therapist. These intersession processes are highly related to the quality of the therapeutic relationship—and especially so when interpersonal and insight-related therapies are employed. Clients

> ...may recreate or replay specific conversations with their therapist between sessions in order to process salient interpersonal lessons, to self-soothe, or to cope with negative events. Additionally, clients may apply lessons learned in therapy, such as trying new coping skills or behaving differently with others.... (Owen, Quirk, Hilsenroth, & Rodolfa, 2011, n.p.)

In one large study conducted in an extensive practice-based research network (Castonguay et al., 2010), researchers found that the two elements in their psychotherapy that were most conducive—most helpful to the clients—were awareness and the therapeutic relationship. That is solid evidence for the effectiveness of two of gestalt therapy's major tenets—a phenomenological approach aimed at increasing awareness (see Chapter 4) and the dialogical approach aimed at facilitating a therapeutic relationship (see following section). In another example of the relevance of gestalt therapy processes, Muran, Eubanks-Carter, and Safran (2010) employed a brief relational approach to psychotherapy for personality disorders and used a quasi-gestalt therapy method that emphasized the two-person field (see Chapter 6), awareness work, and the therapeutic relationship.

THERAPEUTIC RELATIONSHIP IN GESTALT THERAPY

Gestalt therapy relies on the thinking of Martin Buber with the belief that all living is meeting, and that, largely, this meeting can be accounted for in the relational attitudes described by Buber, namely, I–It or I–Thou relational stances (Mann, 2010). I–It interaction is goal oriented, objectifying, and concerned with getting things done. I–Thou interaction is subjective, arises out of a state of being, and is concerned with knowing and being known. Both are needed in life, let alone in clinical practice.

Furthermore, in gestalt therapy terminology, this meeting is called contact, and it results in being in touch with whatever is emerging in the current moment of one's experience (Yontef & Jacobs, 2007). "The central fact of human life, as well as the lives of all organisms, is *contact*, understood as meetings of various kinds with others" (Crocker, 1999, p. 18). The interest in gestalt therapy in field dynamics leads to an interest in the relationship among the various elements in the field. It is a focus on our relative relation to the environment. We call this meeting an encounter or a dialogue, but what it is, basically, is contact. Joel Latner described contact as follows:

> Contact can be described in terms of its distinguishing characteristic, its location, and its primary dimension. Its distinguishing quality is the meeting of differences. It's location we call the contact boundary, and the fundamental organizing quality of contact we call figure/ground. (Latner, 2000, p. 22)

People experience contact by looking, listening, touching, talking, moving, smelling, and tasting (Polster & Polster, 1973). It's a matter of extending oneself to be seen, heard, touched, smelled, tasted, and so on, and it's a matter of hearing, touching, smelling, and so forth another person. In fact, one does not experience contact with an "other" except in the response of the self.

For instance, I was scheduled to present at the Roots of Gestalt Therapy conference in Rome, Italy, and I was presenting on the thinking of Karol Wojtyla (Pope John Paul II), because he was a phenomenological philosopher as well as a Catholic priest, and gestalt therapy is a phenomenological approach. I was also interested in theistic spirituality in gestalt therapy, so the two interests coming together in this one man made him compelling to me, but I was a bit concerned about the reaction of other people. In fact, one of the conference organizers, a very well-known and respected man, asked his co-organizer one day, leading up to the conference, "Are you ready for the Pope?"

As I presented my workshop, I held Wojtyla's book, *The Acting Person*, in my hand and I talked about it. I told people why I thought it was important. Afterward, the skeptical organizer approached me and asked if he could see the book. I handed it to him, and he sat down with it. A moment later, I glanced over to see how he was doing, and he was engrossed in considering it. I felt seen, because this man took an interest in my interest. The moment of contact was in the asking for the book, the handing of the book, the consideration of the book, and the observing of the consideration—all of that. The organizer and I met one another, and I experienced him in a different way. Before that contact, he had been an esteemed grandfather of gestalt therapy, but in the contact he called out to me with a leveling interest, and I felt privileged to be able to respond to him. It was a small thing, but it was a genuine thing. Contact is like that. It can be a big bang or a small snap.

Gestalt therapists attend to the way in which people navigate the contact boundary, which, aside from the place where contact takes place, can be thought of as the relationship between the person and the situation (MacKewn, 1997). People can avoid contact or break contact. It would be considered wise to break contact with an abusive person; however, when people habitually restrict or refrain from contact during the normal course of relational events, that is usually not satisfying. In studying the typical way in which a person navigates the boundary, one can usually find that any given person develops his or her own style of contacting. In tasting, they reject the novel flavor. In hearing, they deflect and listen selectively. In breaking the contact that would lead to novel experience, the addicted person can project, deflect, retroflect, form a confluence, or retreat into egotism. These are all classic gestalt resistances[1] that are used as a first-order response to virtually any stimulus by an addict to avoid spontaneous contact. Table 5.1 lists several of them and includes summary definitions.

Bringing together these concepts, Hycner and Jacobs (1995) wrote that the I–Thou moment is a special occasion of illuminated meeting in which the two persons confirm one another as unique beings. The I–Thou moment is

> the most intense moment of what Polster and Polster (1973) call a contact episode. Any experience of an I–Thou moment is a confirmation of the possibility of integration and wholeness, a confirmation of the learning process by which a person can restore his or her relation to the world. (Hycner & Jacobs, 1995, pp. 54–55)

Relationship is contact over time. Yontef and Jacobs (2007) wrote that contact, speaking of the relationship between the client and the

TABLE 5-1
Contact Interruptions

Contact Style	Working Definition
Introjection	Taking into one's system objects from the environment without assimilating/digesting them
Confluence	Two people (two aspects of the field) flow together with no differentiation
Retroflection	Doing to, or for, oneself what one would like to do to, or with, others or the environment
Deflection	A turning aside from direct contact with people or aspects of the environment
Desensitization	Numbing oneself to sensations in the body or to external stimuli
Egotism	Slowing down spontaneity through excessive introspection, self-vigilance, and intellectualizing so as to avoid social criticism
Projection	Denying or repressing a quality or feeling and attributing it to others—can also refer to the interpretation of experience that is attributed to others or aspects of the environment
Hardening	Stiffening against the presence of another or against other stimuli in the environment

Developed from MacKewn (1997, p. 27).

therapist, is an essential pillar of gestalt therapy. They claimed that in a good therapy relationship, the therapist contactfully attends

> to what the patient is doing moment to moment and to what is happening between the therapist and the patient. The therapist not only pays close attention to what the patient experiences but also deeply believes that the patient's subjective experience is just as real and valid as the therapist's... (Yontef & Jacobs, 2007, p. 347)

Dialogue is the discourse of relationship (Brownell, 2010) and critical to working with addiction from a gestalt perspective (Matzko, 2007). It emerges out of the dialogical attitude as the therapist practices presence, acceptance, and commitment to the process.

In presence, a person enters the circle of contact. It takes a conscious effort to make those steps that comprise entering such a circle. Think of a campfire at night. From a distance, there is a sphere of light that seems contained by the darkness. As one approaches the campfire, the images loom larger and larger until, suddenly, one realizes that he or she is close enough to the fire and within the influence of the light sufficiently enough to no longer need to be able to "see in the dark."

The light of contact blocks it out and one is present in the light, visible to others in the light, and vulnerable to those still outside in the darkness. It takes courage to step into the circle of contact and make oneself visible. It is safer to remain in the darkness, but in the darkness there is no real connection, only groping around and an ambivalence about stepping into the light. Being present means more than simply being with; it means being available, open, authentic, and self-disclosing in a fully embodied way (Mann, 2010). This will include one's physical, cognitive, affective, relational, contextual, and spiritual dimensions. It will mean showing up *on the outside* as one knows oneself *on the inside.* To be present is to be "focused on the here and now, to be aware of oneself, and to bring the self into the therapist/client encounter" (Melnick, Nevis, & Shub, 2005, p. 110).

Acceptance also covers what some call inclusion. Inclusion takes place when the therapist honors the phenomenality of the client without losing touch with his or her own. Both the subjective experience of the client and that of the therapist are "included," and in the process, the client's way of making him- or herself present is acknowledged. Thus, if a client presents in a stiffly distancing fashion, then that is how he or she steps into the light. If the client enters the circle of contact in a wilting and victimized stance, *that* is how he or she does it. The therapist includes his or her own experience, and that is what provides the chance for contact to take place. This is like entering the sphere of light at the campfire and then suddenly seeing another person emerge from the darkness. Suddenly, there is no one else in the perceptual field and one can either open up to the other or break the pending contact in some way.

That is when the therapist needs to remain committed to the process. Commitment signals that whatever the quality of the process, the therapist is committed to dialogue and to creating those conditions in which dialogue might take place.

Dialogue is not necessarily just talking going on between two people—like a variation on a monologue. People can chat up one another at a party, and all the while they can be thinking of somewhere else they'd like to be, and someone else they'd like to be with. The quality of contact on such occasions is poor. Thus, people can talk but not form a satisfying connection. In dialogue, there is contact, and the attitude of the people in question (I–It or I–Thou) goes a long way toward furnishing the raw material for a dialogical moment to take place.

Dialogue takes place within the embodied, co-constructed field also known as the nonindependent dyad (Kenny, Kashy, & Cook, 2006), the social network (Christakis & Fowler, 2009), the field (O'Neill & Gaffney, 2008), or the situation (Robine, 2010, 2011). See Chapter 6 for an understanding of the field, but suffice it to say here that the dialogue between therapist and client does not take place in a vacuum, and what the client and therapist bring into their encounter from outside of therapy includes the worlds of other people (Wheeler, 2000); it often has an important influence on the outcomes of therapy.

Dialogue can also be understood as the meeting of two individual experiences. Thus, it is common that during a dialogical process, the therapist can be seen employing a modified phenomenological method, tracking the client's phenomenality and reporting back on the therapist's experience of being with the client. This process often deals with the shame of relapse, the faulty cognitive patterns associated with "addictive thinking," the difficulty processing emotions, and the client's intersession experiences. Because dialogue is inherently unpredictable and not scripted, the dialogical relationship is itself experimental (see Chapter 7). The venue of dialogue is the immediate encounter between the therapist and the client, incorporating aspects of mindfulness and acceptance in the process. Often, instead of talking about things that have happened "out there," the client and the therapist explore current thoughts, feelings, and purposes—what happens "in here."

Gestalt therapists have usually elevated the dialogical attitude, correlating that to the I–Thou stance in relationship, while stressing the values of authenticity and presence. However, we also recognize that without attending to an I–It stance, no business would get done, and that would not allow the therapist to remain providing service. The research cited earlier, furthermore, indicates that there is substantial benefit to the identification of goals and the tracking of progress with regard to those intentions during the ongoing process of therapy. Contact, which is fundamental to dialogue, is intersubjective and aggressive (Houston, 2003),[2] and that means the client and therapist are open to one another, attend to the business of therapy, and care about making progress. The client expects that progress will be made, and it is impossible to evaluate whether any progress has been made unless one has goals that are measurable in time and space. This would be especially important to those in recovery, because addictions work is not brief therapy, and people need the encouragement of accomplishment.

LISA

Lisa entered the session with a reserved affect. She had a polite smile on her face, she carried herself lightly on her feet, and she sat on the couch, but she did not sit back. She perched there like a bird.

The therapist welcomed her. He sat back in his chair and looked at her.

Lisa did not meet his eyes. She looked across the room just past his left shoulder. Her elbows rested on her knees, and she held her own hands rubbing her fingers tightly with her thumbs.

The therapist said, "I feel a bit anxious, Lisa, because you look to me as if you're about ready to fly away."

Lisa turned her eyes to look briefly at him and then looked away again. She said, "That's what I feel like!"

"You don't want to be here?"

"I don't know what to talk about. On the way up here I was thinking, 'What are you going to say?' and I just came up blah."

The therapist did not say anything. He kept his eyes on her while her own eyes darted back and forth between him and the other side of the room. The silence was demanding, like a party where people forget how to make small talk.

Lisa said, "Aren't you supposed to be giving me advice or something? Why don't you speak up?"

"I'm thinking you really don't want me to give you advice."

"Well I want something. I don't think I can do this on my own. C'mon, doc, you're the shrink. Don't you have a trick up your sleeve so I can get this done and over with?"

"I don't think it works that way. I know I don't have any tricks. What I'm offering is a place—here—and a person—me. I'll meet as often as you need me to."

"Isn't there a pill I can take for this? I've heard there's a pill that will make you sick if you drink."

"Is that what you want?"

"No! I want to be able to drink."

"Then you'd probably find a way to do it, even with those pills."

"How many cures do you have under your belt, doc?"

"You mean like scalps I can boast about?"

Lisa looked at him and smiled. She had stopped rubbing her fingers so tightly with her thumbs. She shifted her weight and leaned back into the couch. She took a deeper breath, and she looked for a longer moment at the therapist. "How are you going to keep me from drinking?" she asked.

The therapist sighed. He smiled softly and said, "I'm not. I can't keep you from doing anything you really want to do."

"Oh great! Then I'm all alone?"

"Are you alone right now? Do you feel alone right now?"

Lisa looked puzzled.

The therapist said, "Do you feel alone right now?"

Lisa looked a little longer at the therapist. She seemed to puzzle over him. Her eyes were not darting away. She took in the features of his face. "No," she said.

The therapist asked, "What is it like for you to be here with me right this moment?"

Lisa was slow to respond. She finally said, "I think you care and mean well."

"Okay, that is what you think. What does it feel like?"

"It feels like custard pudding."

The therapist laughed loudly and naturally. "Nobody ever said that before!" he told her.

She smiled. Her eyes sparkled. Then she said, "I hate custard pudding."

The therapist laughed again. "I don't believe you," he said.

By that time they were both sustaining eye contact; Lisa's affect had brightened and showed more texture and sharpness. She said, "So, is it possible for me to come more than once a week?"

"Well, if we do that," said the therapist, "what are we going to talk about?"

"Are you poking me?" she asked. "Are you making fun of me?"

"Hey. I was there with you in the silence. Remember that? Silence makes me itchy. What was that like for you?"

"I was about to scream!"

"Yeah. That sounds uncomfortable. You're not there now though, are you? What's the difference?"

"I don't know. We just started talking and then it got easier to keep talking."

"And I noticed that you told me you wished all this business about not drinking could be easier. I'm remembering the last time we talked and you doubted whether or not you could succeed."

Lisa's eyes starting glistening. The skin around her lips tightened. The skin across her forehead wrinkled. Then a tear rolled down one of her cheeks, and she tried to speak, but her voice was suddenly raspy and she could not get a word out. She put her face into her hand.

The therapist waited, and there was silence in the room broken only by Lisa's sobbing. After a moment, the therapist said, "I touched something?"

"I'm scared. I could lose a lot."

"I agree," he said. "Would you be willing to commit yourself to trying?"

She nodded.

"Okay then," said the therapist, "here's the deal: both of us will try. Is that good enough for today?"

Lisa said, "That's it? Both of us will try?" She was looking at him a bit wide eyed, waiting to hear that surely there was something more to it.

"No guarantees, Lisa. But if we don't give up, I believe you can make it."

NOTES

1. These resistances, also called "interruptions," have positive uses as well. Through projection, one extrapolates to solve a problem. Through retroflection, one pulls back from a situation that lacks support. Through confluence, one makes love.
2. Aggression in gestalt therapy can be understood as an active pursuit of one's figures of interest, and so most assuredly includes goals and the progress in fulfilling them.

REFERENCES

Bedi, R., & Richards, M. (2011). What a man wants: The male perspective on therapeutic alliance formation. *Psychotherapy: Theory, Research, Practice, Training.* Advance online publication. doi: 10.1037/a0022424

Brownell, P. (2010). *Gestalt therapy: A guide to contemporary practice.* New York: Springer Publishing.

Castonguay, L., Boswell, J., Borkrovec, T., Zack, S., Barker, S., Boutselis, M., et al. (2010). Helpful and hindering events in psychotherapy: A practice research network study. *Psychotherapy Theory, Research, Practice, and Training, 47*(3), 327–344.

Christakis, N., & Fowler, J. (2009). *Connected: The surprising power of our social networks and how they shape our lives.* Boston: Little, Brown and Company.

Crits-Christoph, P., Gibbons, M. B., Hamilton, J., Ring-Kurtz, S., & Gallop, R. (2011). The dependability of alliance assessments: The alliance-outcome correlation is larger than you might think. *Journal of Consulting and Clinical Psychology, 79*(3), 267–278.

Crocker, S. (1999). *A well-lived life: Essays in gestalt therapy.* Cambridge, MA: Gestalt Institute of Cleveland Press.

Horvath, A., Del Re, A., Flückiger, C., & Symonds, D. (2011). Alliance in individual psychotherapy. *Psychotherapy, 48*(1), 9–16.

Houston, G. (2003). *Brief gestalt therapy.* London, England: Sage.

Hycner, R., & Jacobs, L. (1995). *The healing relationship in gestalt therapy.* Highland, NY: The Gestalt Journal Press.

Kenny, D., Kashy, D., & Cook, W. (2006). *Dyadic data analysis.* New York: The Guilford Press.

Kolden, G., Klein, M., Wang, C-C., & Austin, S. (2011). Congruence/genuineness. *Psychotherapy, 48*(1), 65–71.

Latner, J. (2000). The theory of gestalt therapy. In E. Nevis (ed.) *Gestalt therapy: Perspectives and applications,* pp. 13–56. Cambridge, MA: Gestalt Press.

MacKewn, J. (1997). *Developing gestalt counselling.* London, England: Sage.

Mann, D. (2010). *Gestalt therapy: 100 key points & techniques.* New York, NY: Routledge.

Matzko, H. (2007). *Addiction, resistance, forgiveness & treatment: A clinician's guide to addiction treatment from the perspective of a gestalt therapist.* Cranston, RI: Gestalt Institute of Rhode Island.

Mee-Lee, D., McLellan, T., & Miller S. (2010). What works in substance abuse and dependence treatment. In B. Duncan, S. Miller, B. Wampold, & M. Hubble (Eds.), *The heart and soul of change: Delivering what works in therapy* (2nd ed., pp. 394–417). Washington, DC: American Psychological Association.

Melnick, J., Nevis, S., & Shub, N. (2005). Gestalt therapy methodology. In A. Woldt & S. Toman (Eds.), *Gestalt therapy history, theory, and practice* (pp. 101–115). London, England: Sage.

Muran, J., Eubanks-Carter, C., & Safran, J. (2010). A relational approach to the treatment of personality dysfunction. In J. Magnavita (Ed.), *Evidence-based treatment of personality dysfunction: Principles methods, and processes* (pp. 167–192). Washington, DC: American Psychological Association.

Norcross, J., & Lambert, M. (2011). Psychotherapy relationships that work II. *Psychotherapy, 48*(1), 4–8.

Norcross, J., & Wampold, B. (2011). Evidence-based therapy relationships: Research conclusions and clinical practices. *Psychotherapy, 48*(1), 98–102.

O'Neill, B., & Gaffney, S. (2008). Field–theoretical strategy. In P. Brownell (Ed.), *Handbook for theory, research, and practice in gestalt therapy* (pp. 228–256). Newcastle, England: Cambridge Scholars Publishing.

Owen, J., Quirk, K., Hilsenroth, M. J., & Rodolfa, E. (2011, May 23). Working through: In-session processes that promote between-session thoughts and activities. *Journal of Counseling Psychology.* Advance online publication. doi: 10.1037/a0023616

Polster, E., & Polster, M. (1973). *Gestalt therapy integrated: Contours of theory and practice.* New York: Brunner-Mazel.

Robine, J-M. (2010, June 5). *The id of the situation*. Conference presentation at the 10th Biennial Conference of the Association for the Advancement of Gestalt Therapy, Philadelphia, PA.

Robine, J-M. (2011). A background to "the field." *Gestalt!*, *11*(1). Retrieved June 15, 2011, from http://www.g-gej.org/11-1/robine.html.

Webb, C., DeRubeis, R., Amsterdam, J., Shelton, R., Hollon, S., & Dimidjian, S. (2011). Two aspects of the therapeutic alliance: Differential relations with depressive symptom change. *Journal of Consulting and Clinical Psychology, 79*(3), 279–283.

Wheeler, G. (2000). *Beyond individualism: Toward a new understanding of self, relationship, and experience*. Cambridge, MA: GIC Press/Analytic Press.

Yontef, G., & Jacobs, L. (2007). Gestalt therapy. In R. Corsini & D. Wedding (Eds.), *Current psychotherapies* (8th ed., pp. 328–367). Belmont, CA: Thompson Brooks/Cole.

6

The Sense of the Situation

This chapter explores the gestalt therapy tenet of the field, in which all things having effect in the current moment for the client are considered relevant and dealt with in a strategic fashion. This may include memory of the past, for instance, the coping strategies of childhood or adolescence that are no longer adequate. This may also include anticipation of the future, including aspirations and hopes, consequences, and dreadings. This includes the strategic experimentation with disciplines that affect and alter the relapse cycle and influence relationships as well.

Once there was a famous comedian who did a routine on the Ed Sullivan show. I watched it when I was a child, and I can recall laughing. I'm sure a lot went right over my head; however, at one point, with perfect timing, the comedian's punch line came through: "Everybody's got to be some place." And that is it. The issue of the field in gestalt therapy concerns being situated, which is a matter of place in time. Not only *is* everybody some place, but that place also provides a unique perspective on events in people's lives. What one finds is that one's place in time orients one's organization of the field based on need and/or interest.

Describing several basic concepts in gestalt therapy, including that of a field, Gai Houston indicated that a gestalt itself is a field of data in which the foreground is relevant to the dominant need, which will be the next thing with which the organism must concern itself.

A gestalt is an organized field of perception, which probably includes bits of the subject's history and aspirations, as well as present circumstances,

set habits, and all else that is operant at that moment. Gestalt formation is in other words an organization of a field, relating to the past,
the future and the environment, to the internal and the external world.
(Houston, 2003, p. 15)

Gestalt therapy's method has long been thought to be phenomenological. However, taking Lewin's lead in conceptualizing field as not
so much a theory but a method,[1] and taking into consideration how the
relational turn in psychotherapy has echoed ideas nascent in gestalt
therapy all along, I am drawn to the conclusion that gestalt therapy's
actual method is a field strategic methodology that incorporates the
phenomenality of clients, the dialogue between persons, and the experimental and experiential nature of the process. All of these things sup-
ply influences that have effects, and Lewin (1951) aptly observed that
the field is all things having effect at any given moment. He called this
the person's life space.

On another note, for years gestalt therapists have asserted that the
dominant method in gestalt therapy is a phenomenological method.
I contend that that is a relic of a one-person psychology that is overly
preoccupied with the individual experience of the client and bent on
augmenting that client's awareness. I do not deny that that is still a primary factor in our approach, and in fact hold it out as one of the central
or core tenets in gestalt therapy theory (Brownell, 2009). However, it
can no longer stand as the primary method. Virtually all gestalt therapists practicing contemporary gestalt therapy admit that everything
is synced up and connected. The client is connected to the therapist,
and they both meet in a place, and there may be other people in that
place, and that place is located in a community. Common factors psychotherapy outcomes research indicates that extra-therapeutic factors
account for 40% of outcomes, and so it is the life space that is the larger
and overarching influence—those influences from outside therapy
that both the client and the therapist bring into session. Techniques
that therapists use, such as the phenomenological method, account
for about 15% of outcomes, but 30% of the results depend upon the
relationship between the therapist and the client.

Gestalt therapists will inevitably realize that to truly escape the one-
person psychology, they must admit to and develop field–theoretical
strategies that can be employed within the dialogical relationship,
which itself must be seen as an element of the biopsychosocial (BPS)
field. One place to begin with this shift of perspective is with Kurt
Lewin himself.

In 1931, Lewin wrote a piece for the *Journal of General Psychology*
that was titled "The Conflict Between Aristotelian and Galilean

Modes of Thought in Contemporary Psychology." This article was reprinted in an anthology of Lewin's writing edited by Martin Gold (1999), titled *The Complete Social Scientist: A Kurt Lewin Reader*. Prior to Gold's anthology, Robert Carson (1996) had used the DSM taxonomy, in the case of schizophrenia, to illustrate the difference between the Aristotelian and Galilean approaches to science by contrasting the one-person phenomenological perspective of the categorical systems in the *Diagnostic and Statistical Manual of Mental Disorders* versus the dynamic field–theoretical explanations found in the analysis of the person in situ—the situation. A one-person psychology follows Aristotle and is concerned with individual experience as a way to understand the essence of objects (the things as they are), whereas the contextualized, field approach follows Galileo and is concerned with the situation as a way to understand principles of science (the way things work). Applied to people more directly, the Aristotelian approach goes to the individual who is having an experience, whereas the Galilean approach goes to the situation that gives meaning to multiple experiences—the significance of the current complex situation for an individual person. This is the approach that is best equipped to bring together and unite the various core tenets of gestalt therapy (focus on individual awareness of subjective experience, focus on the relationship between two people who have met in contact over time, focus on the life space, which is related to the lifeworld [see Chapter 8 for further discussion], and finally, focus on the movement through time in experimental process that turns abstractions into experiential learning [see Chapter 7]).

With regard to addictions work, then, the field approach (the Galilean perspective) would suggest that no person's addiction can be understood in terms of a one-person psychology. The problem is going to involve groups and environmental contexts and movements of people in process over time. Does this necessarily eliminate the disease model of addiction (one person with an illness that people work on using treatments or that the individual recovers from using a program)? Perhaps not—the field perspective is that of the individual in context, the person–environment combination. There is an individual who has an individual experience (who has a disease), exercises choice (responds to the nature of the disease), and who can be held responsible (acts as an agent of change . . . or not). It is just that to really understand what prompts that person to do anything in any particular way, one must consider him or her in context, in situ, as part of a field. Put concisely, the addict's behavior is influenced by the properties of the field in which that addict is behaving (Berscheid, 2003).

Just to stress this a bit further, following Heidegger, Robert Stolorow (2006) claimed people never come to consider something without any presupposition, contemplating a phenomenon simply as it appears (the purely individual experience). Rather, people are thrown into the BPS field (the world) and start with a forestructure, given the hermeneutic situation (the complexity of experience). Thus, they are always trying to make sense of their experience but can do no other than refer to the context of the situation to do so. This is true for people in a therapy session or outside of it. "We are always situated, in situations, in the world, in a context, living in a certain way with others, trying to achieve this and avoid that" (Gendlin, 1978/1979, n.p.).

As addicts, people encounter challenges in such a field, and some of these are expressed cogently by Peter Philippson:

> A person involved in addiction is modulating their relationship to the world in a number of ways. It affects their ability to deal with difficulties in their world, and it also tends to leave them in the company of other addicted people. A problem often encountered in working with people with addictions is that they have a potential for losing their friendship circles, often based round drink or drugs, and of being faced with difficult situations in their lives that they have deflected with the addiction. A further consideration is that they will often have come from a family situation where either the process was to go with the thing that makes you feel more immediately comfortable, or conversely a family situation which was very demanding and they are reacting to it...In all of these ways, the relationship with the therapist, group, AA community or whatever is a vital part of the success or otherwise of the work. (P. Philippson, personal communication, July 7, 2011)

CONCEIVING OF THE FIELD

In gestalt therapy, there have been basically two ways to conceive of the field: as a force field or environment and as a sphere of influence (O'Neill & Gaffney, 2008). It is mostly the sense of environment that one sees, for instance, in the Perls, Hefferline, and Goodman (1951) text. In that version, the person is not an isolated individual, but an organism/environment entity—contextualized.

> ...the only useful method of argument is to bring into the picture the total context of the problem, including the conditions of experiencing it,

the social milieu and the personal "defences" of the observer. That is, to
subject the opinion and his holding it to a gestalt-analysis. (Perls et al.,
1951, p. 243)

They taught, and others have since developed the idea, that the
self forms at the boundary of contact between the organism and the
environment, and that the sense of self is the system of such contacting. The experience of self, the sense of being "me" at any moment,
is a function of the contact I'm having at that time with whatever is
other. Thus, without "other" there is no self, and that is conceived of
as an environmental other, the sociobiological other, which is both
the physical space and the social influence. This sociobiological other
was conceived of as a field theory by Gardner Murphy (1947), calling it a "situation," and Lewin referred to the situation as occurring
in time, using the construct of situational units (1943). With regard
to contact within the situation, Perls et al. (1951) said, "Every contacting act is a whole of awareness, motor response, and feeling—a
cooperation of the sensory, muscular, and vegetative systems—and
contacting occurs at the surface-boundary *in* the field of the organ-
ism/environment" (p. 258). Thus, the brightness of an individual's
figures of interest and the meeting between self and other occur as
situated process and with situated agency that results in situated
experience. This is what is interpreted according to a hermeneutic
phenomenology.

A contemporary and consilient approximation of the field is the BPS
model, which is prevalent in medicine, disability work, addictions, and
virtually all of health care (Brook, 2011; Bruns & Warren, 2011; Ertelt,
Marino, & Müller, 2011; Gatchel & Kishino, 2011; Kelly & White, 2011;
MacDonald & Jensen-Campbell, 2011).

> The BPS approach stresses the importance of a comprehensive, systemic
> perspective on human development and functioning and emphasizes
> a holistic integration of biological, psychological, and sociocultural
> factors when attempting to understand human psychology. (Meyer &
> Melchert, 2011, p. 71)

In contrast to integrative or assimilative psychotherapeutic
approaches, the BPS is more comprehensive. It includes all of human
psychology, from developmental to current functioning, to personality, psychopathology, and behavior or lifestyle change perspectives
like psychotherapy and medication management. The BPS approach
informs the entire treatment process from intake assessment, through
treatment planning, to the implementation of treatment and on to

outcomes evaluation (Meyer & Melchert, 2011). When used in initial intake assessment, it is a way of obtaining a record of influences in the person's field, but it is not, in itself, the field.

Both the BPS and the field approaches are related to nonlinear, complex adapting systems and complexity theory. Thus, a consilient perspective in therapy is the multisystemic approach. Multisystemic therapy has been used extensively in adolescent work and school- and community-based efforts (Clair, Faille, & Penn, 2010; Lyon & Cotler, 2009; Runions, 2008). In an attempt to integrate salient field–theoretical strategies to provide a comprehensive approach to social work, Lundy (2008) used a multisystemic perspective, bringing together the constructs of the therapeutic relationship or holding environment, client self-determination, the BPS perspective, and the person-in-situation.[2] Wilbourne and Weingardt (2007) identified multisystemic therapy as an evidence-based approach to working with alcohol use disorders.

The multisystemic approach is a way of coordinating with other service providers so as to intervene in the world of the client. It represents one way of moving beyond a one-person psychology, and it also provides a way of moving beyond the dyad of the client–therapist to reflect an appreciation for the complexity of any given situation. In addictions work, the therapist might find him- or herself working with an MD or psychiatrist for medication management, corrections or parole officers, an employer or school official, and/or a spouse or other family members. All of these kinds of people would have effects in the client's life but would not necessarily be physically present in any given session. Thus, the BPS model is useful to provide a ground against which to understand the manifest presentation of the client at any given moment, and the multisystemic approach provides one way of working with the field.

FIELD–THEORETICAL STRATEGY

The configuration of the current field includes memories from the past and expectations of the future; it includes unfinished business that nags for completion as well as foreboding and anxiety, anticipation, and current delight. Many gestalt therapists hold to the idea that people can only know a phenomenal field (Mann, 2010), that is, what it's like for them to be alive at a time in a place. They would say that the external reality, the ontic field, cannot be known; yet, it is precisely that which is in reference when people speak of contact in an environment or contact with another person. There is a real other person in such contact, and the alterity of Emmanuel Levinas (1999; and those following him) demands respect for that other person, whom he elevates to the "other," by which he signifies the transcendent "other" who defies our thematizing, our verbal representations of our encounter. Thus, there are two aspects to a person's field: the subjective sense of being "me" (the phenomenal field) and the objective influence of an "other" (the ontic field). The ontic field is experienced as a condition of being thrown into a world with others; it is a given and a prereflective starting place for the interpretation of experience. Just as countertransference (what comes up in the therapist as a consequence of contact with the client) is a pathway back to the client's dynamics, so the response of the therapist to the call of the "other" is one way of discerning the ontic presence and influence of his or her client. We know the call of the ontic "other" in the response of the phenomenal self (Chrétien, 2004).

Following Lewin (1943), the direction and velocity of change are helpful considerations in contextualizing the phenomenality of the client. In terms of direction, the question is "where does this come from?" Lewin was interested in causality. The therapist pursues his or her curiosity about what any particular phenomenon might be related to. Although a scientist would be interested in causality, accurate causality is too elusive, but correlation is manageable. The therapist follows the way in which a client does whatever he does: "I notice that when you talk about your father, your voice tightens up." This is one way in which a modified phenomenological method serves the more comprehensive construct of a field–theoretical strategy (Brownell, 2010; O'Neill & Gaffney, 2008). In the same way, the therapist follows the call of the client, which is sensed in the subjective experience *of* the client, which can be self-disclosed through dialogue, and the discourse of such dialogue can be either verbal or nonverbal. That is, the therapist can say, "Your tears move me," or the therapist can allow him- or herself to be moved and to manifest that through the body—the therapist's face can fall in sadness and tears can form in his or her eyes. In this way a dialogical moment serves the field–theoretical correlation, "Where did this come from?" Often, when a therapist is attuned to the client and the call of the client's world correlates to the response in the therapist's world, the reciprocal loop in turn has an impact on the client, and he or she can "see" it in the therapist, who is "other" for them. Thus, without analytic exercise, or thematizing, the simple but profound contact with a situated "other" can lead to openings. In terms of speed, the question concerns moments of shift and the relative potency or "speed" with which they come, and it concerns the overall pace of the therapeutic process. Significant change in psychotherapy is often associated with peak moments of emotional processing, which is not simple catharsis, but associated with increasing awareness of emotion, expressing emotion, enhancing emotion regulation, reflecting on emotion, and transforming emotions with emotions (Greenberg, 2008).

As implied previously, working a field–theoretical strategy requires that one "move" on the client's field from one's position in it. This could mean responding to something sensed or felt, to a "hunch" picked up in the presence of the client. This was aptly described by O'Neill and Gaffney (2008) when referring to an image of gloves that kept coming to the attention of a particular therapist while talking with his client; after attempting several times to bracket it away, the therapist acknowledged it by saying something like, "Pardon, but while I've been listening to you the image of a pair of gloves has kept pushing its way into my awareness. Does this have any meaning for you?" Where upon the client expressed sudden excitement and began to speak with vividness about her father (and the process took a productive turn right there).

Moving on the field could also mean using a unilateral experiment (see Chapter 7) in which the therapist initiates some action that provokes a response in the client. The therapist might express disappointment, sadness, anger, or other emotions in response to something in the client's narrative. This would be an intentional act, actually becoming the disappointment, the sadness, or the anger that corresponds to those words, and letting the client experience them in the embodied therapist.

This could involve the therapist contacting other stakeholders in the client's case[3] to coordinate care, and even calling a case conference in which the client and/or his or her family were present.

This could be the taking of a rigorous history, including genogram or sociogram. If the field is all things having effect, then asking probing questions becomes necessary. This is nowhere more vividly illustrated than when working with offenders who are reluctant to talk about their offending histories. They require layers upon layers of interview and dialogue to uncover patterns in their offending that they deny or minimize. It is I–It conversation, with a goal of retrieving information that provides a web of meaning. The same is true for people in addiction who often live in a shadowy semi-awareness of what they are doing, and the task is to stay with them, burrowing beneath the superficial level of dialogue to get at some "facts." Incidentally, it is this effort to understand more of the client's field that prompts me to invite the parents of adolescents in for the first meeting, because parents provide another perspective on the situation, and if I go with the adolescent alone, I am often stonewalled by that young person's trivializing, deflecting, or simple blindness. If both parent and child are in the room at the time, we negotiate what people are there for, and it allows the work to proceed from that point with an awareness of the parental perspective. I have often found myself later saying to the adolescent who has told me that everything is fine, "What would your mother say if she were sitting on that couch?" It helps that she *has* sat on that couch saying what is wrong and what she wants to see changed. That first meeting becomes an artifact of the young client's field.

Table 6.1 summarizes various field–theoretical strategies available to the therapist.

TABLE 6-1
Field–Theoretical Strategies

Strategy	Description
History, including the use of devices like a genogram, to assess the biopsychosocial field	Gathering historical and developmental data/facts relevant to the client's life
Moving on the client's field through dialogue-based self-disclosure experiments	Being with the client (practicing presence) and self-disclosing through action what one is experiencing in the presence of the client (includes both verbal and nonverbal discourse)
Multiple perspectives	This is the input from a spouse, parents, siblings, teachers, other service providers, fellow employees, and/or supervisors
Moving on the client's field through the following of hunches	Allowing what is nascent in the mix between therapist and client to "bubble up" to awareness just enough to be acted on in the form of following a hunch
Multisystemic approach	This is the purposeful consultation with other stakeholders and service providers so as to coordinate care
Attending to direction	Asking oneself where some particular behavior "comes from," the correlations among aspects of the process
Attending to pace	Keeping mindful of the velocity and the potency of the therapeutic process

GILBERT

Gil was all day getting to the residential treatment center he had selected. It took catching an early flight from Bermuda, laying over in New York for a couple of hours, and then catching another plane out to the west coast of the Unites States. He had started off with the best of intentions of not drinking on his way, but he got into the airport at 6 p.m. Pacific time, which was 10 p.m. Bermuda time. He was exhausted, and he wanted a drink; however, someone from the treatment program met him as he emerged from the security section on his way to the bar. Disappointed in himself, because he knew quite well what he had intended to do, and frustrated with the situation, because he had not been able to do it, Gil was not pleasant.

It took another hour to get to the treatment program, and by that time, Gil was also hungry. He had not eaten since he left New York. He had just missed dinner at the treatment facility; so, when the intake process began he suddenly blurted out, "Hey! You guys got any food in this place?"

Now, as it happened, the staff member who was doing the intake was on the second leg of a double, because someone else had called in sick. That was okay, because he told himself he could use the double time, but he was beginning to get a bit tired. Having gotten dinner out of the way, he knew there was one group he still had to conduct and then it would be time to suggest lights out for the residents, the TV would go off, and hopefully there would be no crises on the unit that night. He could kick back and chat with his friend, the charge nurse. Then, they got this man named Gilbert who was raising his voice aggressively and demanding to be fed.

The staff member grabbed a couple of containers of apple juice and tossed them to Gil. He said, "We'll see about getting you something to eat after we get some information, but the chow has already come and gone and the kitchen people have probably already shut down."

"Well, shit man. Why don't you call down to the kitchen and see if you can get something now, and then I'll answer your questions."

The staff member and the charge nurse looked at one another. She said, "I'll take care of it." She picked up the phone and called the kitchen. Then she turned to Gil and the staff member and said, "a tray will be set aside for you. Get done with this and then we'll send someone down there to get it. Shouldn't take long."

Gil rolled his eyes. "Okay then. Let's get on with it!"

They took his vital signs. They asked a lot of background questions. What did he do for a living? Had he ever had a serious accident? Was he using any substance besides alcohol. Where did he live? Bermuda? What's it like in Bermuda?

At that point he said, "Are you kidding me? What am I a travel agent?"

They told him the psychiatrist would be by soon to see him, and they took him into his room. They searched his entire luggage, right down to the spaces in his shoes and the lining of his suitcase. They searched him as well, and they insisted that he take off all his clothing to do it.

> "What the hell!" He complained. "Do you think I've got a bottle in my pants?"
>
> They took his container of razor blades, saying that they were a danger to other residents. They took a package of cigars. They took his lighter. They took his MP3 player, saying he would not need its distraction. They took his laptop and cell phone for the same reasons. They took his watch and they took his rings and gold chain because they said they might get stolen.
>
> "Where are you putting these things?" Gil began to complain. "I'm getting serious now. I'm gunna get bored out of my skull in this place!"
>
> The staff member brought him a pair of blue, cotton pajamas and told him to get into them. He could stay in his room instead of going to group, and the psychiatrist would be by to see him soon.
>
> "What about dinner?" asked Gil.
>
> "I have to run group now. I'll ask the charge nurse about it. You can just lay down and take a rest. You've had a hard day."

Outside, just down from his door in the hallway, Gil heard the sound of keys in a door, and he stepped to the door of his room. That's when it hit him that he was on a locked unit. He went back to his bed and sprawled across it. This was not at all what he had expected. Now he was locked up, and he was starting to feel the need to have a drink, not just the desire, but the need.

About 15 minutes later, Gil came to the nurses' station, and he was visibly trembling. He was angry. He yelled at the charge nurse and threatened to leave the place if he didn't get some food. He pounded the wall. He marched back and forth. He told another patient who had noticed him to mind his own business. The charge nurse and one of the therapists confronted him and told him to go back to his room and wait for the psychiatrist. They also told him that if he got any louder and threatening, especially to other patients, they would have to lock him up in a quiet room. They reminded him that he signed a voluntary commitment when he arrived and that now he was their responsibility. Again, they told him to go back to his room.

> He did. He sat on the edge of his bed for another 10 minutes before he heard keys in the door down the hall from his room. The psychiatrist arrived in his room with a chart, and he said, "Hi, I'm Dr. Martin."
>
> Gil answered, "Well skippedy doo. I'm Santa Claus!...No, seriously, doc, it's about time!"
>
> Dr. Martin sat down on the bed across from Gil and looked Gil over. He said, "When was the last time you had anything to eat?"
>
> "Ha! This morning...Bermuda time! And it's like midnight there now!"
>
> Dr. Martin said, "Come with me," and he took Gil out of his room and to the locked doors in the hall. He put his keys in the lock, unlocked the doors, and he told the staff person, "It's okay. I'll take him." He turned to Gil, and he said, "Come on."
>
> Dr. Martin took Gil down the corridor, around a corner on the next unit, out to the doubled doors that lead into the administration department, and then through some more doors, around another corner, and through some further doors where Gil found himself in the kitchen of the hospital. "Let's see what we can find here for you to eat," he said.
>
> "Yeah?" said Gil, very surprised. "What would you do if I just ran off right now?" He asked.
>
> Dr. Martin said, "Where ya gunna go? We've got your wallet, your watch, whatever stuff you had...we've got it, and you're far away from Bermuda. Where ya gunna go?"
>
> Gil said, "Fair enough. What are we going to do here?"

"It's a kitchen, and you need something to eat. Can you make a sandwich? I'll find some bread and stuff." Between the two of them they looked around the kitchen and found what they needed. While Gil chomped away on the food and drank some water, Dr. Martin asked him various questions. He did a simple mental status examination. He felt his skin. He took his pulse, and he told him to stop chewing long enough to listen to his heart and lungs. As Gil finished up the food, Dr. Martin wrote in his chart, including orders for a benzodiazepine to take the edge off his withdrawal and some vitamins. He ordered that staff take his vital signs periodically through the night and that he be monitored closely, then he said, "Okay, let's get back to the unit."

Once back behind the locked doors again, and back in his room, Dr. Martin waited while the staff prepared the first dose of medications, and he went over his orders with the charge nurse. Then, he told Gil he'd be seeing him the next day. He told him that he had also written orders for Gil to see the psychologist for an assessment and the nutritionist to go over the diet that he'd be on while at the program. He said he would also meet with the social worker who would handle all the paperwork and such; Gil had arrived after hours for administration, and they'd need to catch up. "So, tomorrow will still be a bit chaotic," he said, "but we'll get it sorted out." Then, he left.

> The charge nurse arrived at Gil's bed to administer the medications, and Gil said, "Now there's a doctor."
> The charge nurse noted the difference in his affect, and she said, "You must be feeling better."
> "Yeah," he admitted. "Sorry if I was rude before. It's just like, have you ever traveled from Bermuda to the West coast?" They both laughed.
> The charge nurse told him they'd be in every hour to take his pulse, check his breathing, and taking his blood pressure. "It'll be rough, but you'll make it." Her attitude toward him had changed. She saw what she thought was fear in his eyes, and she remembered why she got into the line of work she was in. She said, "These pills should help you sleep too."
> As she turned to go, she had a thought. It seemed to come to her from somewhere else, and she realized she usually would not think that thought twice. However, this time she had a hunch that it might be relevant. She said, "Have you called your wife to let her know you made it here okay?"
> Gil suddenly looked as if he'd been shot with a stun gun.
> "Well," said the charge nurse, "I guess that says it all. Come with me...and don't tell anyone." She took him to the nurse's station, got an outside line, looked up Gil's wife's number in the intake information, and dialed it in. Then she handed him the receiver.
> "Hi, honey, it's Gil." He looked up and smiled at the charge nurse. He whispered toward her and with his silent lips, saying, "Thank you."

NOTES

1. This is how Lewin put it in "Defining the 'Field at a Given Time'" (part of his book on field theory in the social sciences, p. 201): "Field theory, therefore, can hardly be called correct or incorrect in the same way as a theory in the usual sense of the term. Field theory is probably best characterized as a method: namely, a method of analyzing causal relations and of building scientific constructs. This method of analyzing causal relations can be expressed in the form of certain general statements about the 'nature' of the conditions of change."

2. This represents the sense that core elements in the gestalt approach are relevant to effective practice. The therapeutic relationship or holding environment is related to a dialogical relationship, client self-determination is related to the experience of self at the boundary of contact, which can be followed through a modified phenomenological method, and both the biopsychosocial perspective and the person-in-situation are reflective of gestalt's field methodology.
3. Obviously with previous client consent for release of information that allowed for consultation with others as stipulated.

REFERENCES

Berscheid, E. (2003). Lessons in "greatness" from Kurt Lewin's life and works. In R. Sternberg (Ed.), *The anatomy of impact: What makes the great works of psychology great* (pp. 109–123). Washington, DC: American Psychological Association.

Brook, D. (2011). Group therapy. In M. Galanter, & H. Kleber (Eds.), *Psychotherapy for the treatment of substance abuse* (pp. 277–298). Arlington, VA: American Psychiatric Publishing, Inc.

Brownell, P. (2009). Gestalt therapy. In I. Marini, & M. Stebnicki (Eds.), *The professional counselor's desk reference* (pp. 399–407). New York: Springer Publishing.

Brownell, P. (2010). *Gestalt therapy: A guide to contemporary practice.* New York: Springer Publishing.

Bruns, D., & Warren, P. (2011). Assessment of psychosocial contributions to disability. In P. Warren (Ed.), *Behavioral health disability: Innovations in prevention and management* (pp. 73–104). New York: Springer Science.

Carson, R. (1996). Aristotle, Galileo, and the *DSM* taxonomy: The case of schizophrenia. *Journal of Consulting and Clinical Psychology, 64*(6), 1133–1139.

Chrétien, J. -L. (2004). *The call and the response.* New York: Fordham University Press.

Clair, M., Faille, L., & Penn, J. (2010). Prevention and treatment of violent offending/offenders. In C. Ferguson (Ed.), *Violent crime: Clinical and social implications* (pp. 351–377). Thousand Oaks, CA: Sage.

Ertelt, T., Marino, J., & Müller, A. (2011). Etiology of compulsive buying. In A. Müller, & J. Mitchell (Eds.), *Compulsive buying: Clinical foundations and treatment, practical clinical guidebooks* (pp. 19–26). New York: Routledge/Taylor & Francis Group.

Gatchel, R., & Kishino, N. (2011). The biopsychosocial perspective of pain and emotion. In G. MacDonald, & L. Jensen-Campbell (Eds.), *Neuropsychological and health implications of loss and exclusion* (pp. 181–191). Washington, DC: American Psychological Association.

Gendlin, E. (1978/79). Befindlichkeit: Heidegger and the philosophy of psychology. *Review of Existential Psychology & Psychiatry: Heidgger and*

Psychology, 16(1–3). Retrieved July 7, 2011, from http://www.focusing.org/gendlin_befindlichkeit.html

Greenberg, L. (2008). Emotion and cognition in psychotherapy: The transforming power of affect. *Canadian Psychology, 49*(1), 49–59.

Houston, G. (2003). *Brief gestalt therapy.* London, England: Sage.

Kelly, J., & White, W. (2011). Recovery management and the future of addiction treatment and recovery in the USA. In J. Kelly, & W. White (Eds.), *Addiction recovery management: Theory, research and practice (Current clinical psychiatry)* (pp. 303–316). Totowa, NJ: Humana Press.

Levinas, E. (1999). *Alterity and transcendence.* New York: Columbia University Press.

Lewin, K. (1943). Defining the "field at a given time." *Psychological Review, 50*(3), 292–310.

Lewin, K. (1951). In D. Cartwright (Ed.), *Field theory in social science: Selected theoretical papers.* New York: Harper.

Lundy, M. (2008). An integrative model for social work practice: A multisystemic, multi-theoretical approach. *Families in Society, 89*(3), 394–406.

Lyon, A., & Cotler, S. (2009). Multi-systemic intervention for school refusal behavior: Integrating approaches across disciplines. *Advances in School Mental Health Promotion, 2*(1), 20–34.

MacDonald, G., & Jensen-Campbell, L. (Eds.). (2011). *Social pain: Neuropsychological and health implications of loss and exclusion.* Washington, DC: American Psychological Association.

Mann, D. (2010). *Gestalt therapy: 100 key points and techniques.* New York: Routledge.

Meyer, L., & Melchert, T. (2011). Examining the content of mental health intake assessments from a biopsychosocial perspective. *Journal of Psychotherapy Integration, 21*(1), 70–89.

Murphy, G. (1947). Field theory. In *Personality: A biosocial approach to origins and structure* (pp. 880–902). New York: Harper.

O'Neill, B., & Gaffney, S. (2008). Field–theoretical strategy. In P. Brownell (Ed.), *Handbook for theory, research, and practice in gestalt therapy.* Newcastle, England: Cambridge Scholars Publishing.

Perls, F., Hefferline, R., & Goodman, P. (1951). *Gestalt therapy: Excitement and growth in the human personality.* London, England: Souvenir Press.

Runions, K. (2008). A multi-systemic school-based approach for addressing childhood aggression. *Australian Journal of Guidance and Counselling, 18*(2), 106–127.

Stolorow, R. (2006). Heidegger's investigative method in Being and Time. *Psychoanalytic Psychology, 23*(3), 594–602.

Wilbourne, P., & Weingardt, K. (2007). Therapeutic outcome research and dissemination of empirically based treatment for alcohol use disorder. In P. Miller, & D. Kavanagh (Eds.), *Translation of addictions science into practice* (pp. 259–276). New York: Elsevier Science.

7

The Willingness to Experiment

This chapter explores the gestalt therapy tenet of experiment, which is a move from talk to action. This is what gestalt therapy is most often associated with, an experiential method of intervening. However, the "safe emergency" of experiment is more open ended than that. Experiment is a way of making more clear and crisp one's figures of interest and experience of self, leading to creative adjustment and paradoxical change. In recovery, there is no predetermined outcome from a given intervention; one tries something out to adapt and adjust one's individual lifestyle and to make one's recovery program a unique solution.

The experiential nature of gestalt therapy is probably at once the most frequent association people make to it and the most misunderstood—that and they believe gestalt is also largely about confronting people. These things are far from the truth, of course. As Carmen Vasquez Bandin (2011) noted, "Gestalt therapy, whose primary objective is the expansion of a person's *awareness*, is characterized above all by its use of *experiments* ..." (p. 57), and it is to the understanding of experiment that I now turn.

THE ESSENTIAL EXPERIMENTAL NATURE OF GESTALT THERAPEUTIC PROCESS

Although not a widespread opinion, some gestalt training organizations do not regard experiment to be one of the core theoretical tenets in gestalt therapy. They submerge it into phenomenal awareness work, seeing experiment as a technique that does not rise to the level of a methodology. In their description, they speak of experiments becoming fixed and "canned."

Contrary to that opinion, the fundamental nature and unpredictability of the gestalt process are experimental and therefore experiment exceeds the scope of a technique. The move to action facilitates a revealing that accords with the essential nature of gestalt therapy as being an existential and phenomenological approach. "Field" in gestalt therapy is a method, not a theory, and experimental action is necessary to a field methodology. Finally, the core of gestalt therapy praxis, including experiment, forms a natural unity.

Gestalt Therapy Process Is Experimental

The fundamental nature and unpredictability of gestalt process are essentially experimental and therefore exceed the scope of a technique. Both the basic gestalt process and experiment are built on action in the current moment that reveals persons and establishes experience of self (Roubal, 2009; Wojtyla, 1979). Joel Latner noted:

> Much of the practice of gestalt therapy consists of a careful examination of contact, the creation and destruction of figures (creative adjustment), and the experiential dimensions of these. The part of gestalt theory which concerns itself with these as attributes of the individual is called the theory of the self. (Latner, 2000, p. 41)

Experiment is richly creative and artistic, based on the aesthetic criterion (Bloom, 2003), "If you speak about experiment I think you have to consider this part of our theory: otherwise you miss a fundamental part of the art of doing experiments" (Gianni Francesetti, personal communication, May 23, 2010). That assertion also applies to the fundamental part of the art of doing therapy itself; they are of the same fabric. Gestalt therapy uses a creative balance between a human therapeutic relationship and a more active, task-oriented approach, through which the therapist influences the process more directly (moving on the field) and thus helps deepen the client's experience (Roubal, 2009).

For example, in terms of case conceptualization in gestalt therapy "diagnosis is an hypothesis about contact, containing an experiment that enables its own evaluation; diagnosis and therapy are identical" (Bloom, 2003, p. 68). Furthermore, case conceptualization is a collaborative process resting on the quality of contact (Francesetti & Gecele,

2009) in which both client and therapist develop criteria for change (Yingling, 1998) over time that can only be described as tentative, negotiated, and emergent. It is experimental.

As such, it rests on the uncertainty of a faith position intrinsic to all gestalt process, which is predicated on the characteristics, and the caliber, of contact in the environment. Perls, Hefferline, and Goodman (1951), the founders of gestalt therapy, said, "... faith is knowing, beyond awareness, that if one takes a step there will be ground underfoot; one gives oneself unhesitatingly to the act, one has faith that the background will produce the means" (p. 343).

Thus, faith becomes an instrument of knowing and an essential principle of contact. Stepping into the circle of contact, making oneself present, takes trust. People exercise trust every day, but at a low level; at the market, they purchase produce they believe has been handled properly. In this they suspend disbelief and extend trust. At the theater, people expect that what is advertised, and what they bought their tickets for, will actually be what they experience when the curtain goes up. People trust the process of life as they find themselves in the current of it. Just so, faith is a basic instrument of experiential knowing in the processes of contacting, which, at times like being in therapy, can feel like a very high level of trust. Faith is a basic starting point of the support required to establish and maintain contact. Both the therapist and the client trust that if they take a chance on being present and committing to the process, that they will find ground underfoot.

The definition of an experiment in gestalt therapy differs from what it is in experimental psychology. "A gestalt therapy experiment is a purposefully created experience in the support of increased awareness that facilitates change; it is unpredictable ..." (Brownell, 2010, p. 155). Yontef and Jacobs (2007) described experimentation as trying something new to increase understanding. "The attitude for experimentation in gestalt therapy is 'try something new' and be aware, notice what you experience" (Yontef & Philippson, 2008, p. 271). Put in a common vernacular, one might say, "Let's try this and see what happens."

Beyond that understanding, however, experiment in gestalt therapy can be understood as a basic modality of therapeutic work (Kim & Daniels, 2008). Jennifer MacKewn (1997) linked experimenting to learning through active participation and action research: gestalt experiments "... involve the exploration of the client's experience through active, behavioural or imaginative expression rather than merely through internal cognizing or verbal explanation" (p. 133). Peter Philippson (2001) regarded experiment as included in the concept of dialogue, and Gary Yontef (1993) regarded experiment as a means of gaining insight into the structure of the field and of a person's processes of awareness.

These observations link experiment with the other three core tenets of gestalt theory. However, experiment is not simply linked to a core; it is *essential to* and therefore part of that core. Yontef and Philippson (2008) asserted that gestalt therapy is designed for the creative use of phenomenological experimenting, carried out within a dialogical relationship that addresses the enduring or repetitive processes of the client as they naturally occur in the flow of contemporary experience.

> Each moment in gestalt therapy is considered a moment of creative contact and creative phenomenological focusing and experimenting, in which the twin poles of the autonomous person that endures over various contexts and the self-actualizing person that is created anew in each moment can be explored. (p. 257)

One essential feature of experiments is that they are paradoxical. That is, the experiment is in the service of increased awareness and understanding, but where one client or another might take an experiment is a function of the situated context—the relationship between the individual person and the relative field of which he or she is a part, which varies from case to case. It cannot be known ahead of time and the basic rule of the experiment, as it is in gestalt therapy as a basic process, is to remain in the moment to find out—as it were to support the uncertainty that each step in the present moment brings.

> We create the conditions for growth to occur without having any commitment to a specific outcome. The commitment is to create a climate that allows the client opportunities to explore and to discover his or her experienced awareness rather than following a direction imposed by the therapist. (Melnick, Nevis, & Shub, 2005, p. 107)

Experiments cannot be prescribed like medicine to achieve predetermined results. In this regard, what is said about experiments is identical to what is said about the paradoxical theory of change that is fundamental to all of gestalt therapy process. In fact, it can be argued that the paradoxical theory of change is an axiomatic expression recognizing the core status of the experimental in gestalt therapy. Arnold Beisser (1970) stated that a gestalt therapist encourages the client to be whatever he or she is experiencing in the current moment. Fundamental to this perspective is the belief in classical gestalt therapy that internalized conflicts and polarities can be resolved by encouraging the client to identify with all aspects of his or her self-functioning, and experiments, the concrete and time-limited expressions of this basic perspective, are created to facilitate these kinds of integrations. Even more fundamental and relevant to the issue at hand, the therapist is most helpful when he or she can be him- or herself while in intimate contact with the client. This is like hanging onto the tail of a tiger; let go and it will eat you, but hang on and you've got the most exciting ride of your life. That is what makes gestalt therapy, all of its process, a "safe emergency," and these bounded outgrowths, these things we have identified as experiments, are simply its most tangible and easily identifiable eruptions. Someone who does not understand the experimental nature of all of gestalt process might see such concrete manifestations, sense they were separate from gestalt process, and call them techniques. However, as Laura Perls (1992) claimed, "Gestalt therapy is an existential, experiential and experimental approach...The basic tenets of Gestalt therapy are philosophical and aesthetic rather than technical. Gestalt therapy is an existential-phenomenological approach and as such it is experiential and experimental" (pp. 131, 149).

Experiment Is Existential and Phenomenological

Experiment offers a way of testing the limits of a person's subjective experience, illuminating the self, and paradoxically "stretching" and informing regarding the boundaries of a person's authenticity.

The move to action facilitates a revealing that accords with the essential nature of gestalt therapy as being an existential and phenomenological approach. As stated above, the experimental contact in gestalt therapy is supported by existential faith. It was Kierkegaard who posited a kind of faith that is personal, exposing the authentic self through the action in which any given person engages. Karol Wojtyla (1979) claimed that people disclose themselves through action, and that when someone acts, he or she becomes the agent of that action while that action becomes another form of discourse (Wolterstorff, 1995).

> ...being/person is to consciousness as action/acting is to experience. Discourse depends on someone actually existing with whom conversation might be established, but once being is accepted, then the person is manifest in action. When a person acts, he or she self-actualizes and communicates a potential in some way, to some extent, to other beings, and that is discourse. Thus, when a gestalt therapist moves from talk to action, it is not really a move from one category to another but from one aspect of a single category to another. Both talk and action are forms of discourse. The related action in experiment helps bring into clearer relief who the person is by what he or she does. (Brownell, 2010, p. 154)

One of the emphases in gestalt therapy, what gestalt therapists can do, is the tracking of a client's phenomenal field—the following of that person's unfolding phenomenality. The modified phenomenological method, which is not really what Husserl imagined in his philosophical writings, is a philosophical process turned on its head to serve a therapeutic purpose (Bloom, 2009; Burley & Bloom, 2008), and it is actually more accurate to view it as related to a field methodology. This is because when someone observes something, he or she affects the things observed, shifts the direction of the process (what Lewin would have called the vector in the situational moment), and that whole process becomes part of "all things having effect"—the life space or the field. So, in one very important and basic sense, the "phenomenological method" is one form of experiment. It might be said that a therapist asks, "What might happen if I observe, bracket, and describe right now?" Whenever he or she does so, it constitutes a unilateral experiment (see the section entitled Bilateral and Unilateral Experiments).

Experiment Is Necessary to a Field Methodology

As we have established, "field" in gestalt therapy is a method, not a theory, and experimental action is essential to a field methodology. Kurt Lewin addressed the common construct of a "field theory" claiming that it was not essentially a theory as much as it was a method. He wrote,

> *Field theory is probably best characterized as a method:* namely, a method of *analyzing causal relations and building scientific constructs.* This method of analyzing causal relations can be expressed in the form of certain general statements about the "nature" of the conditions of change. (Lewin, 1943, p. 294)

> Whereas Lewin conceived of field theory as a way of conducting research, gestalt therapists utilize field theory as a way of doing psychotherapy. As such, it shares kinship with the conceptualization of complex, adaptive systems and is consilient with family systems and group therapy as well as with organizational dynamics for people with large groups or groups within organizational systems. (Brownell, 2010, p. 120)

In a field methodology, what the therapist does, the enactments of the therapist, affect the relationship between therapist and client as well as the subjective experience, the phenomenality of the client. This is not a unidirectional process, for the client influences the therapist as well, but when we are talking about an approach to doing therapy, then as therapists we are concerned with what the therapist does. One of these things could be to listen openly to the client in a dialogue, but another thing the therapist might do is to suggest a bilateral experiment—all of which would actually be experimental because it would be unpredictable and ultimately uncontrollable.

In a field methodology, for instance, those extra-therapeutic factors that account for approximately 40% of outcomes (Brownell, 2008; Duncan & Miller, 2000) are not simply facts to know about the client or the situation. The gestalt field perspective is not a passive process designed to think about the situation as much as it is, as Lewin asserted, a means by which to affect change. It employs a paradoxical theory of change, but a gestalt field perspective is an active approach—a move from knowing to acting. One is not simply collecting facts *about* the field; one is moving on and working *with* the field.

If one were to read the various categories of experiments in Kim and Daniels (2008) or Brownell (2010), one would see that these are activities. Furthermore, if one consults the case presentation in O'Neill and Gaffney (2008), one immediately senses the experimental nature of the field–theoretical strategy used, what someone uninitiated might call "playing a hunch," but what is actually a very sophisticated use of the field in meeting the client and getting to half-realized, shadowy awarenesses in the ground of the meeting between client and therapist. It is a picture of a two-person field in action.

The Core of Gestalt Therapy Praxis Is an Unbroken Unity

If you take one of the four elements of phenomenality, dialogue, field, and experiment *out* of gestalt praxis, you not only cannot use the others but you will also no longer *have* the others. That is, shine the laser of gestalt process through the prism of the field and what comes out in a spectrum on the other side is phenomenality, dialogue, and experiment. Likewise, shine that light through experiment and what comes out is field methodology, dialogue, and phenomenality. You can do this with each of these four core constructs. They are intrinsically linked to one another through a therapy of contact. If two people are working with the contact between them, they are presenting their experience and tracking the experience of the other in a modified phenomenological fashion, engaged in dialogue, and manifesting themselves as influences in the field of the other.

> Gestalt therapy theory is unified by constructs that endure across its four main tenets and mold them into a framework that is both solid

and dynamic. Theories of self, contact, and action, as well as theories of health and change abide whether one is focused primarily on the phenomenological method, dialogic relationship, field theoretical strategies, or therapeutic experiments. Every time there is a phenomenological inquiry it takes place between people, in the context of a relationship, and involves contact. Because the meeting between therapist and client is alive, it is therefore to some extent unpredictable and experimental. The therapeutic situation thus provides both therapist and client opportunities to practice behaviors that are improvised to fit *this here-now* situation—a skill that is essential to living authentically and well in the everyday situations of life. (Crocker, 2008, p. 143)

It is precisely because gestalt therapy's core provides a unified system that it is also unifying, what many have described as assimilative. To be both unified and unifying, a system of psychotherapy would have to accomplish the following:

- Emphasize the essential function, structure, and processes common to all human systems
- Establish the interconnectedness of all the domains of human functioning
- Shift to a metatheoretical model or total paradigmatic matrix
- Offer a theory of the functioning of the entire ecological system of human functioning, including all pertinent areas of psychology, especially psychopathology or maladaption, personality theory, developmental processes, as well as psychotherapeutic processes
- Recognize all the major domain systems of the human biosphere
- Acknowledge the personality system as central to organizing of human adaptation, function, and dysfunction
- Rely on multiple paradigms for knowing, holding that each holds some value that deepens understanding

(Adapted from Magnavita, 2008, p. 275)

Gestalt therapy is a holistic system offering an emergent view of self that comprises what other systems know as personality, that is, the organizing of subjective experience with a metanarrative about the identity of the person in which both move through time and space, syncopated by the evolving situations in which the person exists. This includes the relational considerations in the working alliance as well as intimate systems such as couples and families, and it extends to teams and large configurations within organizations. It is the same view as that of relational systems psychoanalysis, which illustrates gestalt's comprehensive ability to pull together constructs from various clinical paradigms. A similar consilience exists between gestalt therapy and the mindful and constructive elements of cognitive–behavioral therapy. Gestalt is a comprehensive, all-encompassing approach. Gestalt therapy's field methodology includes all things having effect, regardless of what domain or system is in focus, and its philosophical base includes major discussions of epistemology, ontology, and ethics. In terms of a philosophy of science and a scientific method in psychology—systematic observation, mathematical analysis, and conceptual analysis—gestalt therapy provides a solid ground for the third leg of such a method—conceptual analysis (Brownell, Meara, & Polák, 2008). Individual experience is relational, situated, and made manifest through experimental action, which as a whole is indivisible—a unity. This is gestalt therapy.

BILATERAL AND UNILATERAL EXPERIMENTS

If the basic idea of an experiment is trying something out to see what might happen, then a therapist has a couple of options in terms of how to do that. The therapist can negotiate an experiment with the client, or the therapist can simply move to action, doing something while in contact with the client that will require the client to adjust, respond, or otherwise deal with what he or she encounters in the action of the therapist. The first is a bilateral experiment and the second is a unilateral experiment.

In the negotiation of a bilateral experiment, the therapist invites the client to try something out. There is usually some kind of orientation to the experiment in which the therapist provides a kind of informed consent, explaining that there is no success or failure attached, but that often there is new experience to sort through that might be helpful. The last part of the "setup" describes what the therapist has in mind to try out. It is usually simple and concrete; after all, what is proposed is an action, and not a discussion of a theory or an abstraction. Also, because the experiment is in the flow of the process, it is usually couched in a dialogue. It looks something like this:

Therapist: I notice that you wince when you mention your grandmother.
Client: I do?
Therapist: Yes. What is that about?
Client: I don't know.
Therapist: Would you like to try something to see if we can learn more about that?

Client: What do you mean?

Therapist: Call it an experiment.

Client: I suppose. What would we do?

Therapist: You close your eyes and see if an image of your grandmother comes to mind.

Client: Okay. Yes.

Therapist: What is she doing?

In the implementation of a unilateral experiment, there is no negotiation. The therapist simply moves to action. Unilateral experiments emerge from the dialogical process as antecedents to the therapist's clinical curiosity about the client and/or as the authentic response to something the client is saying or doing. They are not done to manipulate the client or to apply a technique to change the client. When employed, a unilateral experiment looks something like this:

Client: [talking at length about the death of a child, the loss of a job, the crippling accident of a brother, and the abandonment by a spouse, all within a year's time, but all described in a flat, matter of fact affect]

Therapist: "That is a lot to go through."

Client: I guess, but one has to put one foot in front of the other, look on the bright side, keep the chin up.

Therapist: [the therapist feels the sadness and the loss, feels compassion for the client, is aware that he could cry if he let it happen, and he decides to let it happen in order to see what the client does with that] All that makes me sad [tears forming in the eyes and spilling over and down his face; he does not wipe them away; he lets them keep flowing].

Client: Oh! [tears now forming in her eyes] It's so awful! Too painful [where upon she sniffs her nose, wipes her eyes, shifts her body on the couch, and collects herself physically, looking away from the therapist].

Therapist: You don't want to see my sadness?

Client: NO! It reminds me of my own and I don't want to be sad. Would you? I do everything I can to ignore it.

AUGMENTING AND DIMINISHING

There are many ways to describe the various experiments that arise during gestalt process. One of the simplest distinctions is between augmenting and diminishing. Simply put, if a therapist notices something the client is doing that seems significant, the therapist can ask the client to do it again, or do it more demonstrably or do it more loudly. On the other hand, if a client has been too intense and overwhelming in his or her presentation, and this seems to be a habitual way of relating to others, the therapist might suggest that the client try whispering, or that the client hold himself or herself back from responding at all for the current moment. While meeting with a couple, the woman broke down in tears and the man reached out to comfort her, starting to talk hurriedly; I put my hand out to him as a stop sign and told him not to say anything. His wife continued to cry and without interruption; so at that moment, I was augmenting one and diminishing the other.

ASSIMILATED TECHNIQUES USED EXPERIMENTALLY

Gestalt therapy provides a rich framework for the assimilation of techniques and practices from other modalities. When that happens, these techniques are not simply applied "straight out of the box." They are chewed up and digested, becoming part of the body of gestalt therapy. However, there is one way in which a person could say that he or she has assimilated various features common to other clinical approaches, and that is, after understanding them, to use them experimentally. Thus, imaginal desensitization can be used by a gestalt therapist, and the ensuing experience can be debriefed with the client. A reframing can be introduced, saying, "What happens if you think of it this way...?" The therapist is not doing that to effect a predetermined result, but rather to explore with the client how the client constructs meaning relative to the dynamics in question. In a kind of completing the loop, strategies and techniques that have been employed by other orientations, but that seem consilient already with gestalt therapy, can be picked up and used. Thus, the various techniques in mindfulness and acceptance therapy, behavioral systems science, existential-phenomenological, and relational psychoanalytic therapies are ripe for the picking because they already really resemble gestalt therapy.

Having said that, it is good to recall that whatever experiential movement the therapist takes with the client, it is not technique driven. The action is consistent with a paradoxical approach, and it arises naturally from the current flow of the therapeutic process and is adapted to it.

HOMEWORK

Having just stressed the current, face-to-face flow of a therapeutic process, here is one adjustment. Homework can be given/suggested and, once again, done so as experiment. What, for instance, happens when an addict is told to contact his physician for a full physical to rule out any conditions that might affect his or her recovery? This could be considered simultaneously a move on the client's field and an experiment. Many addicts first come into therapy denying that they have gotten out of control with their using; a common experiment (verging almost to the point of technique) is to ask the client to remain clean and sober for a period of time so that both he/she and the therapist can learn something about how much control the addict actually has over his or her using. This kind of "homework" is carried out outside the therapy room, in vivo in the addict's world. The results at once affect the recovery process and inform both the addict and the therapist, which leads to still further refinement of the therapy that supports the recovery process.

MELISSA

Immediately after Gilbert left for his residential treatment program, Melissa started feeling lonely and desperate. She went to yard and estate sales trying to fill her days. She had coffee in downtown Hamilton, but the place she chose was where young guest worker families congregated, and they had their babies with them. It made her feel all the more lonely. She found herself eating more while looking over her online catalogues for good buys on jewelry. She did not actually need any jewelry, but there was something about its sparkle and its apparent value that made it seem like she was actually saving money to purchase it at a discount. She didn't think about that too closely. On the first day that she came in to see the therapist, she was feeling anxious because she had not been able to talk with Gil after that first conversation when he'd gotten to the treatment program.

"Hi, Melissa," said the therapist.
"Hi. I'm not doing well."
"What's up?"
"I feel like I'm going to jump right out of my skin! I don't know how to live without him in the house. What's with *that*? I never used to be that way."

"You feel…what? Out of control? Lost? What?"

"I feel nuts!"

"What is 'nuts' like?"

"I can't get organized. I sit around wondering what he's doing, and I have no desire for anything else. I tried calling his cell phone, but he doesn't answer. Sometimes I imagine he's ignoring me. What if he finds someone else at the treatment center. You know, I've heard of such romances."

"Hm. Let's imagine a scale. Can you see it?"

"You mean a bathroom scale?"

"No. I mean the kind where you see Lady Justice holding the scales, and there's two …"

"I've got it."

"Okay. Now, onto one side of the scales put Gil. Can you see him there?"

"Yes. He's just standing there."

"Okay, now, what's on the other side of that scale? Let something emerge."

"A bottle of vodka!"

The therapist laughed. He said, "Well, that makes me think you see that as Gil's scale, but what if it's yours? What if it's about you?"

"Like what's important to me?"

"Could be that. Could just be things that keep coming to your mind."

There was silence. Melissa closed her eyes. The therapist waited.

The air conditioning kicked on and a gentle breeze began to flow into the room. It whistled slightly. A hand on the clock on the table next to the tissues clicked forward one second at a time. The therapist watch Melissa try to find something in the other half of the scale—something to balance the image of Gil.

"Nothing!" she finally said. There's nothing there. Then her face tightened up, and her eyes locked onto the therapist. "This is pathetic," she said. "Without him I'm nothing?"

"Is that what it seems to you? Tell me more. Are the scales balanced?"

"They are balanced, but I just can't see what makes them balanced."

"What's that like?"

"Well, it's a lot better than if they weren't balanced and Gil was the only weight being measured. Guess I'm something, but with him in the picture I can't see me."

"Ah. Can you say that again?"

"What? With him in the picture I can't see me?"

"Say it again."

"With him in the picture I can't see me. With him in the picture I can't see me."

"Now put the accent on the word 'see.'"

"With him in the picture I can't *see* me. I can't *see* me.... Right! I can't see me but I'm there, I am."

They sat in silence for a few moments. She was looking down at the floor, and he was watching her. Eventually she looked up. Her body had relaxed slightly, but her eyes looked alive.

"You seem changed somehow. What's going on with you?"

"Well, the frantic feeling is gone and I feel...*curious!*"

"Curious? About what?"

"About *me.*"

They both laughed.

"Sounds like a project," said the therapist.

CONCLUSION

I propose that the core of gestalt therapy consists of four constructs that are inherent to one another in a unified approach. They certainly did not start off being related to one another, but through a psychotherapy of contact, in which the aesthetic of contact "... emerges from within sensible experience as the sight, sound, touch, and even smell of life" (Bloom, 2003, p. 64), they have become molded and fused to one another. These are phenomenality, dialogical relationship, field methodology, and experiment.

Not all gestalt therapists will agree about all the various aspects of gestalt therapy, and some might say that this or that other construct is just as important. What I contend is that if one practices the core I have laid out here (and does so within the scope of addictions work), the rest of the gestalt pantheon of theoretical constructs and practices will come along, and one will find himself practicing a paradoxical treatment approach to recovery. Practice the core and all else follows—all else, including the emergence of self, the formation of figures of interest, the relationship, and the contacting of organism and environment.[1] Take any of the four away, and you mortally wound the practice of gestalt therapy.

Here, in a more focused argument, I have also maintained that experiment is critical to gestalt therapy because its nature as action undergirds everything else that takes place. I also believe such action accords with the existential and phenomenological roots of gestalt therapy in continental philosophy, and its roots in the German science of Lewin and Goldstein, for experimental process, is essential to a field methodology.

NOTE

1. There has been a great deal written about these and other aspects of gestalt therapy. An exhaustive treatment of gestalt therapy is beyond the scope of this book. The reader is advised to consult the works of Gary Yontef (1993), Peter Philippson (2001, 2009), Margherita Lobb (2005), Sylvia Crocker (1999), Lynne Jacobson (1995, 2010), David Mann (2010), Jennifer MacKewn (1997), Ruella Frank (2001, 2010), Gordon Wheeler (1996, 2000), Talia Bar-Yoseph Levine (2005, 2011), Edwin Nevis (1987, 2000), Gaie Houston (2003), Erving Polster (1973), and the articles in various gestalt-related journals that exist all over the world.

REFERENCES

Bandin, C. (2011). Personality: Co-creating a dynamic symphony. In T. Bar-Yoseph Levine (Ed.), *Gestalt therapy: Advances in theory and practice* (pp. 49–58). New York, NY: Routledge.

Beisser, A. (1970). The paradoxical theory of change. In J. Fagan, & I. Shepherd (Eds.), *Gestalt therapy now* (pp. 77–80). Palo Alto, CA: Science and Behavior Books.

Bloom, D. (2003). "Tiger! Tiger! Burning Bright"—Aesthetic values as clinical values in gestalt therapy. In M. S. Lobb, & N. Amendt-Lyon (Eds), *Creative license: The art of gestalt therapy* (pp. 63–78). Austria: Springer-Verlag.

Bloom, D. (2009). The Phenomenological method of gestalt therapy: Revisiting Husserl to discover the "essence" of gestalt therapy. *Gestalt Review, 13*(3), 277–295.

Brownell, P. (2008). Practice-based evidence. In P. Brownell (Ed.), *Handbook for theory, research and practice in gestalt therapy* (pp. 90–103). Newcastle, England: Cambridge Scholars Publishing.

Brownell, P. (2010). *Gestalt therapy: A guide to contemporary practice.* New York, NY: Springer Publishing.

Brownell, P., Meara, A., & Polák, A. (2008). Introduction and purpose of the handbook. In P. Brownell (Ed.), *Handbook for theory, research and practice in gestalt therapy* (pp. 2–26). Newcastle, England: Cambridge Scholars Publishing.

Burley, T., & Bloom, D. (2008). Phenomenological method. In P. Brownell (Ed.), *Handbook for theory, research, and practice in gestalt therapy* (pp. 151–183). Newcastle, England: Cambridge Scholars Publishing.

Crocker, S. (2008). A unified theory. In P. Brownell (Ed.), *Handbook for theory, research, and practice in gestalt therapy* (pp. 124–150). Newcastle, England: Cambridge Scholars Publishing.

Duncan, B., & Miller, S. (2000). *The heroic client: A revolutionary way to improve effectiveness through client-directed, outcome-informed therapy.* San Francisco, CA: Jossey-Bass, Inc.

Francesetti, G. & Gecele, M. (2009). A gestalt therapy perspective on psycho-pathology and diagnosis. *British gestalt journal*, 18(2), 5–20.

Kim, J., & Daniels, V. (2008). Experimental freedom. In P. Brownell (Ed.), *Handbook for theory, research, and practice in gestalt therapy* (pp. 198–227). Newcastle, England: Cambridge Scholars Publishing.

Latner, J. (2000). The theory of gestalt therapy. In E. Nevis (Ed.), *Gestalt therapy: Perspectives and applications*. Cambridge, MA: GestaltPress.

Lewin, K. (1943). Defining the "field at a given time." *Psychological Review*, 50(3), 292–310.

MacKewn, J. (1997). *Developing gestalt counselling*. Thousand Oaks, CA: Sage Publications.

Magnavita, J. (2008). Toward unification of clinical science: The next wave in the evolution of psychotherapy? *Journal of Psychotherapy Integration*, 18(3), 264–291.

Melnick, J., Nevis, S., & Shub, N. (2005). Gestalt therapy methodology. In A. Woldt & S. Toman (Eds.) *Gestalt therapy history, theory and practice*. Thousand Oaks, CA: Sage Publications.

O'Neill, B., & Gaffney, S. (2008). Field–theoretical strategy. In P. Brownell (Ed.), *Handbook for theory, research, and practice in gestalt therapy* (pp. 228–256). Newcastle, England: Cambridge Scholars Publishing.

Perls, L. (1992). *Living at the boundary*. Highland, NY: Gestalt Journal Press.

Perls, F., Hefferline, R., & Goodman, P. (1951). *Gestalt therapy: Excitement and growth in the human personality*. New York: Julian Press.

Philippson, P. (2001). *Self in relation*. Highland, New York: Gestalt Journal Press.

Roubal, J. (2009). Experiment: A creative phenomenon of the field. *Gestalt Review*, 13(3), 263–276.

Wojtyla, K. (1979). *The acting person: Analecta Husserliana, the yearbook of phe-nomenological research* (Vol. X). Dordrecht: D. Reidel Publishing Company.

Wolterstorff, N. (1995). *Divine discourse: Philosophical reflections on the claim that God speaks*. Cambridge, UK: Cambridge University Press.

Yingling, Y. (1998). *GARF assessment sourcebook*. New York, NY: Routledge.

Yontef, G. (1993). *Awareness, dialogue, & Process: Essays on gestalt therapy*. Highland, NY: Gestalt Journal Press.

Yontef, G., & Jacobs, L. (2007). Gestalt therapy. In R. Corsini, & D. Wedding (Eds.), *Current psychotherapies* (8th ed., pp. 328–367). Florence, KY: Cengage.

Yontef, G., & Philippson, P. (2008). A unified practice. In P. Brownell (Ed.), *Handbook for theory, research, and practice in gestalt therapy* (pp. 257–276). Newcastle, England: Cambridge Scholars Publishing.

III

A Program for Changing One's Life

8

One's World

This chapter describes what a "world" is in phenomenology and describes a person as having a homeworld with many horizons. It defines "horizon" and "attitude," showing how these constructs contribute to a person's world. The chapter concludes by showing how one can purposefully construct aspects of a life, including the building of various disciplines, according to one's attitudes and horizons.

LISA

"I am about ready to go out of my skull," she said.

The therapist smiled. He studied her visually. She was well dressed, and her hair looked freshly done. Her makeup was spot on. Her black hair was cut in whisps with bright mahogany highlights. She carried an iPad in a special case that framed and held it.

She said, "I've got it all together on the outside, but inside I don't know what I'm doing. All I can think to do is go to the club. I've got myself all dolled up like I'm ready to go drinking, but I know if I go to the club, I'm going to drink."

"And if you don't go to the club?"

"Then I don't know what to do with myself."

"What are you interested in?"

"Nothing! Everything I was doing I was doing around drinking. The friends I have all drink; in fact, that's the first thing that comes out when we get together. I can't imagine getting together with anybody because they'll ask me why I'm not drinking."

"Is it a bad thing not to be drinking?"

"Well, no, but...they'll all be getting silly with each other, and I'll be the deadbeat in the group."

"Does alcohol make life fun?"

"Yes, it does!"

"Did you ever have fun before you started drinking so heavily?"

"I don't know. I can't remember what it was like before. Except, I think I felt odd and self-conscious a lot, and that wasn't fun."

"How do you do business deals now that you're not drinking?"

She smiled. "I *am* drinking." Her eyes twinkled and she watched the therapist for his reaction. Eventually, she said, "I'm drinking fruit juice or tea. I still have to have a glass in my hands."

"It's a prop?"

"Yes. Doesn't give me a buzz, but it's better than nothing."

The therapist said, "Makes it rough when you're only interest is alcohol."

She was quiet for a moment. "Are you rubbing it in and telling me I'm a loser?" She looked irritated.

"Just making an observation."

A few moments of silence punctuated that statement.

"And get this," she said, breaking the silence, "when I get home after work, I feel antsy because the first thing I would do before was fix myself a drink. I got rid of the bottles, and it feels like part of me has been cut off. I wander around for a while feeling lost."

"And then what happens?"

"Well, eventually, I just eat something or watch TV. I'm bored to death!"

"Would you like to try something out?"

"I guess."

"Imagine that a long time friend of yours is coming to visit Bermuda. He's never been here before, and he's asked you to put together a list of things to do. What would be on that list?"

She was quick to the task. She said, "Well I'd take him to the Crystal Caves, and then we'd go to Dockyard and visit the Maritime Museum. Of course we'd have to do something on the water, so I'd take him on one of those glass bottom boats that go out to the reef by the shipwrecks."

The therapist was impressed. "That was quick. Anything else?"

"Yeah. Fort Scaur—and we'd eat at The Whitehorse Inn in St. Georges, because I like to sit beside the water and feed the fish that swim right there. Besides, there's the town of St. Georges itself. Gotta do that. "

"Pick one of those things you just told me about and explain why you're friend would find it interesting."

She was quick. "The glass bottom boat."

"What is so interesting about that?"

"He is a movie nut, and they filmed The Deep about that wreck that's out there. So, you can go snorkeling and see it. I think he'd love that."

"Have you ever done that yourself?"

"No."

"Do you like movies?"

"Well, I guess. I used to love to go to the movies, but the movie theaters around here don't measure up."

"Have you ever seen 'The Deep'?"

"Sure. Okay, I get it. So, maybe I'll take myself out for a trip on the glass bottom boat and go snorkeling? All by myself?"

"Let's imagine that you are going to do that. What would be interesting to you about snorkeling out on the reef there and seeing the wreck of The Constellation?"

"Well, I always wondered how far out those boats go...and I've been told the water is very clear out there; I'd like to see how clear. I'd be interested to see the actual place where they set up a shoot to make the movie...and I'd like to see the fish."

"That's a lot of interest. If you had a professional interest, like being a film maker, a fisherman, or something, what kind of a professional person would you be when you went out to view the wreck of The Constellation?"

"I'd be a photographer. In fact, I think I'll buy one of those disposable waterproof cameras to shoot some shots."

"You could go with a 'photographer's mind' then, huh?"

"That's right."

"Why don't you try it out and see what happens? Just notice what's going on. Consider yourself with a photographer's mind who has *got* to see the wreck of The Constellation, and if you want, the next time we talk you can tell me all about it."

ATTITUDE, HORIZON, AND WORLD

In this age when people go up in rockets and circle the globe in space-craft, to speak of the world brings to mind pictures seen from the land-scape of the moon. It's a blue and white spacescape against a black background. It has color and seems almost alive, especially in contrast to the chalky looking moon that is void of life. We live on that planet, and it is our world. People are scattered all around that globe and live in various parts of it. There are many cultures in the world, and we feel the need to be sensitive to them. However, that is not precisely what I am talking about in this chapter. Rather, I'm talking about the concept of a person's lifeworld—that which constitutes the setting for his or her life, and by "setting" I do not mean simply, coming back to that, the physical part of the earth where that person might eat, sleep, and breath in and out.

Remembering that gestalt therapy is an existential and phenomenological approach, it becomes necessary to think about what a few of such concepts suggest about the way people experience things. This is important to working with addicted processes because it so often boils down to simplistic references to things like "stinkin' thinkin'" when so much else is going on that could become relevant to recovery. Hopefully, the following constructs (attitude, horizon, and world)[1] can become handles for people to use to exert some leverage in their work.

These ideas come from the intentionality of Edmund Husserl, augmented by the thinking of Martin Heidegger, who developed the sense of a person as a situated being. While Husserl was interested in knowing things in the world, Heidegger was interested in the relationship things have with people and the significance of elements in one's world relative to human activity and lived experience. "Experience inevitably involves an encounter with an alterity that cannot be reduced to a mere emanation of the constitutive subject" (Jay, 2006, p. 99). Although we are contemplating the perceived, constructed, experienced world of someone else—the client—we are not talking about phantoms and "unreal" kinds of antecedents to a person's experiences. If there were a table in the room, Husserl might be trying to figure out its qualities—its essential features— whereas Heidegger would be seeing that table in its relationship to the people who use it (Inwood, 1997). Just so, those who work with addicted and self-medicating clients are not trying to figure out the nature of the addict as much as they are attempting to enlarge the addict's world.

The significance of one's world is that it is immediately available, and the significance of one's attitudes and horizons is that they are the scaffolding on which one builds the features of one's world. All these things are not simply constructs that people create in abstract absentia from the world but are parameters for the ways in which one experiences and makes meaning of one's experience. We are worlded; our subjective perception of the world and the external reality of the world cannot be separated (Mølbak, 2011). In perceiving a rock, we perceive something in the world, and that links both the subjective perception and the objective/external reality being perceived. Furthermore, we do these kinds of intentional acts because we *are* worlded, because we are situated, and because the starting place for us is the world in which we find ourselves. Husserl works his way into phenomenology by inquiring back from the "pregiven lifeworld " (Husserl, 1970); Heidegger starts off with it (Gendlin, 1978–1979).

These things become important for addicts who typically work with anemic attitudes and restricted horizons. Their world has been shrink-wrapped around the drug of their choice. This dynamic is very important to understand. People are "worlded," meaning that they are all constantly present to the things in this world, and there is a reciprocal relationship between the things (sometimes referred to as objects) and the persons who experience those things (referred to as subjects). In one sense, the objects call to the subjects, revealing themselves, but in another sense, only the subjects can give meaning to the objects. Thus, if you picked up a stone and rubbed your thumb across it, what would it feel like? As soon as you realize what it feels like, you also realize the impact the stone has had on you, such that you picked up *that* stone and such that the experience of it was what it was—and as soon as you say what it feels like, you have given meaning to that stone. You would not have done so if the stone had not called to you in some way. Consider music. Music, an object, reveals itself to the subject as a change in the subject, which the subject does not experience outside of his or her response; the object is not simply a thing in itself, because it is only known in the way a person interacts and responds to it (Chrétien, 2004; Mølbak, 2011). One starts tapping the foot, swaying, or rushing to turn it off. Until one receives the "call" of music, it is simply background noise that evokes no response, and one does not really know it. This ability to block out objects that might call to us is at the crux of the centrifugal nature of addictive experience. It is the shrinking of one's world such that one's world gets wrapped around the drinking, drugging, and self-medicating behavior. According to gestalt therapy terminology, it is the reduction of a normal cycle of experience to sensation and action (Clemmens, 2005).

Attitude

The word "attitude" can be understood variously. One can have a "bad" attitude. One can have a "pleasant" attitude. Seen that way, attitude is mostly about what others think of one's mood or state of mind. The most common understanding of attitude is that of a settled way of thinking or feeling about something or someone. Such an attitude colors the way people see their surroundings, the events taking place around them, and the people who cross their paths.

Attitude from a phenomenological perspective—and thus applicable to the practice of gestalt therapy, a phenomenological approach—is somewhat different.

As mentioned previously, need or interest organizes the life space of an individual—that person's field. So, let's go further with that. People are never simply passive in the way they do what they do. They move on their fields with interest (Luft, 1998). If I am hungry, I see a grocery store as a place where I can get something to eat. If I am a designer, I see the grocery store as an expression of someone's creativity and sense of efficiency. If I am an artist, I see that grocery store as a potential object for one of my paintings. Conversely, if I am hungry, I am less likely to see the grocery store as an object of art.

The attitude is the atmosphere we breathe; it envelops us and affects how we perceive. It is the scent one carries and the tint through which one sees the things around. The attitude organizes one's perceptions according to a central interest.

One of the things I frequently suggest to people is that they explore scent shops and places where they can sample fragrances with the idea that they are looking for a fragrance that will create a positive, soothing, settling proprioceptive (inner) experience. It's something they can play with, and the results are entirely relative to each person—it's an experiment. As such, it is a suggestion as an experiment for handling anxiety, but what that results in for a person is not an ascription like, "That is sweet"; it is not simply a thought in one's head but a whole-person experience in one's core that often also has a feeling tone. The scent abides in one's system and continues to affect the whole person. It can provide a corrective experience because it tends to hold the person experientially, like an atmosphere that engulfs and surrounds. So, in one sense, an attitude is a holding environment in a state of mind. In another sense, an attitude is the tint through which one views what is around. If the tint is green, one sees things as green. One does not see the redness of things. One can only appreciate and have perceptual room for green.

Others have described the attitude as a halo around one's interests, such that specific focal points of interest might change, but while in a given attitude, all subsequent focal points would share or have the same basic interest. The way of perceiving would be consistent across these various cases of interest.

In the therapeutic attitude, I might see my client as in need of help emotionally, and I might be given to various ways of responding. One after another, I would see my clients, and they would each evoke a slightly different, yet still interesting, therapeutic response. Then, if I were to step out of session, but remain in the therapeutic attitude,

I might become interested in, and tend to view, comments by the building inspector as pathological, and I might begin psychologizing that person.

An addict is perpetually in the addictive attitude. The color he or she sees is infused with activities related to drinking and/or drugging. Friends and associates are considered in terms of how useful they can be for obtaining and using the drug of choice. Activities of life are increasingly seen to be drug related. Life is structured to conform with that dominant interest, and contextualized events are interpreted in accord with the attitude, so that meaning is drug related and dependent on the way one sees what is going on.

Horizon

Horizon can be thought of as all things held possible for a given world, and for each attitude there is a horizon and a corresponding world. When one's horizon is closed, not much is believed to be possible, and one's possibilities seem slim. It's as if there is an unfolding scroll with everything possible listed on it, and if something is not there, the person simply never thinks of it. A person in such a condition also experiences a dearth of creativity. On the flip side, a person whose horizon is open and expansive enjoys vivid, spontaneous, and wide-ranging creativity, the horizon is constantly expanding, and that person's possibilities seem almost limitless. A corollary to this idea from the domain of personality theory, and in particular that personality trait called "openness," describes a useful continuum:

> Openness to Experience is defined as the proactive seeking and appreciation of experience for its own sake, and as toleration for and exploration of the unfamiliar. This domain contrasts curious, original, untraditional and creative individuals with those who are conventional, unartistic, and unanalytical. (Piedmont, 1998, p. 87)

In the Big Five approach to personality, openness comprises six subscales: fantasy (vivid imagination), aesthetics (appreciation for art, beauty, design), feelings (receptive to inner feelings and emotions/ views emotion as important to life), actions (willingness to try different activities, visit new places, or eat different foods), ideas (intellectual curiosity), and values (readiness to reexamine social, political, and religious values).

An example comes from the Food Channel, where shows featuring various chefs are presented. One, in particular, features two chefs who compete with each other to create dishes using some kind of "secret" ingredient. If this is not a living, breathing analysis of the horizons of these various people, chefs and judges both, then I don't understand what I'm talking about. These people have to imagine new ways to put flavors together, cook them, and present them on the plate in a way they believe might please the judges, and the judges in return have to respond. When they do, they give themselves away with regard to the status of their horizons.

Let me explain this from a different perspective. The horizon is not just a Procustean standard. A Procustean standard serves as a comparison against which other things can be evaluated. Procustes, in mythology, stretched people to fit his bed, or in another version, cut parts of them off to fit a shorter bed. A horizon does not work that way. The horizon is simply all things that seem possible or come to mind and accord with a given attitude. There is no comparison. If something is not found in the chef's horizon, he or she does not even think of it (let alone think of it to stretch it or cut it off). Thus, when the chefs compete to demonstrate their ingenuity with regard to the secret ingredient, they demonstrate the relative ranges of possibilities that occur to each of them.

> The openness one has toward potential objects encountered in any given attitude is called the horizon that correlates to that attitude, and for each horizon there is a corresponding world. Thus, for the business attitude there is a horizon/world of business. For the designer's attitude, there is a horizon and world of design. The objects encountered in these attitudes and worlds exhaust a person's attention so that one is unaware of the given attitude or the given world as such, even as they act like channels that steer one's considerations. In gestalt therapy this is called identifying with one's figure of interest. In addition, the total influence of one's culture and society create a grand horizon and its corresponding world, and that is called the individual's *homeworld*; the homeworld is what provides one's sense of normalcy such that objects and experiences are either considered normal or alien by virtue of their relationship to the homeworld. (Brownell, 2010, p. 88)

The point here is not that there are such fixed personalities but that people have these capacities. To think in these terms opens up avenues for experimentation for the therapist attempting to work with any number of horizons for an addicted client.

World (Homeworld/Lifeworld)

This idea of a world is variously conceived of, and written about, in the literature. The world is the natural setting for our lives. It is at once the ground of our knowledge of anything in life and the place where we encounter and use the things in our lives. It's our physical neighborhood—but more than that, it's the mindscape we inhabit. If your life were a story, your world would be the unique setting of that story. It is the correlate of our possible experiences (Moran, 2000).

Each attitude comes with its own horizon and world. Thus, the designer's attitude and horizon correspond to the designer's world. The musician's attitude and horizon correspond to the musician's world.

Figure 8.1 shows one way to conceptualize the relationship among the attitude, the horizon, and the world. Looking at it this way, the dimensions of the horizon influence the attitude, and both of them determine the scope and quality of the world.

The same person might have several worlds that he or she inhabits, each with its own horizon and attitude. These are not separated chambers in a person's life; rather, they overlap and interpenetrate one another. The person moves from one attitude and world to another during the course of a day. Any given person usually has many. As already noted, taken together, all these worlds comprise a person's lifeworld or homeworld.

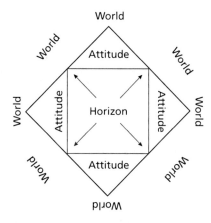

FIGURE 8.1   Relationship Among Horizon, Attitude, and World

The universal notion (Inbegriff) or field of this structure of attitudinal multiplicity and the correlative horizons in my natural life as a whole Husserl calls homeworld[2] (Heimwelt). By this he means the sphere in which we feel "just natural," at home and at ease. Hence this homeworld is not one world of a single individual, but an intersubjective world, a world of tradition, culture, religion (myths), collective values, i.e. a phenomenon of generativity. It is the world we are, literally, accustomed to. Therefore, this homeworld is the world of a certain family, society, people, nation with their historical tradition. (Luft, 1998, pp. 158–159)[3]

It is the homeworld that provides the sense of me/not me, and it is the lifeworld that provides overall influence. These are not mutually exclusive but are two ways of viewing something that may be the same thing. Certainly, something that is "me" or "not me" and is in my life such that I take notice of it is affecting me.

APPLICATION TO ADDICTIVE PROCESS

As stated previously, the addict's world is diminished by the addiction. The person becomes preoccupied with the drug of choice—rituals are formed around its procurement, its funding, its preparation, and its use. Behavior becomes compulsive, and the time that could have been used to explore other things in life gets spun to the periphery.

By the time most chemically dependent clients reach treatment, the self-administration of drugs is often the only source of pleasure in their lives. Either family, social, or recreational activities have been given up, or the drug us [sic] been incorporated into them. (Thombs, 1994, p. 221)

As expressed in Figure 8.1, the horizon contracts, pulling the attitude with it, and the addict's world shrinks. The center of his or her world is filled with substance use and/or self-medicating behaviors and the rituals associated with them, but increasingly little else. Other things are not found in the horizon and so are not simply rejected; they never occur to the mind.

The addict operates almost exclusively with a self-medicating attitude. Thus, recovery must include more than mere sobriety. Recovery must include the salvaging of several rather dormant worlds, the expansion of their horizons, the enrichment of their attitudes, and the enlargement of the lifeworld. This can be seen as a field–theoretical strategy that comes right out of a basic phenomenological orientation.

The lifeworld is the ground of the life space. The person is situated in both, attempting to use whatever is at hand to make his or her way in the world. Even scientists, who play with the inquisitiveness that prompts them to inquire into the things themselves, do so in the only space that is available to them at the time—call it life space or lifeworld, it amounts to pretty much the same thing. Seen from the perspective of someone who intends to move on the field and use the means available, it is the lifeworld. Seen from the perspective of someone who is moved on by the field (and influenced by its various features), it is the life space.

As the addict progresses through the stages of recovery, more worlds emerge, prompted by interest, held in the halo of attitude, and encouraged by the growing possibilities in horizon. Thus, what starts off at the level of a residential treatment center with the world of using and the world of an introjected recovery program (learned through participation in the programs of that center) grows, on returning home, to include the world of a 12-step support system. If it remains just at this level, however, it is still an anemic lifeworld, a limited life space, and something that does not support long-term recovery. Don't misunderstand; it can support long-term sobriety, but in order for long-term recovery to develop, the client will need to continue entertaining interests, birthing new worlds, and braving the individuation of his or her recovery program. That is the focus of the rest of this book.

NOTES

1. The reader can also find treatments of these concepts in Brownell, 2010, pp. 82–88.
2. Husserl also uses the term "lifeworld," and so this is part of the confusion one encounters around the construct of a world.
3. It is notable here that a convergence of some sort seems to take place in contemplating some constructs from Lewin, Husserl, Heidegger, and Merleau-Ponty. "Life space," "lived world," "worldedness," and "lived body"—do these things not orbit around the same sun?

REFERENCES

Brownell, P. (2010). *Gestalt therapy: A guide to contemporary practice*. New York: Springer Publishing.

Chrétien, J-L. (2004). *The call and the response*. New York: Fordham University Press.

Clemmens, M. (2005). *Getting beyond sobriety: Clinical approaches to long-term recovery.* Cambridge, MA: Gestalt Press.

Gendlin, E. (1978–1979). Befindlichkeit: Heidegger and the philosophy of psychology. *Review of Existential Psychology and Psychiatry: Heidegger and Psychology, 16*(1,2,3). Retrieved June 15, 2011, from http://www.focusing.org/gendlin_befindlichkeit.html

Husserl, E. (1970). *The crisis of European sciences and transcendental phenomenology: An introduction to phenomenological philosophy.* Evanston, IN: Northwestern University Press.

Inwood, M. (1997). *Heidegger: A very short introduction.* Oxford, England: Oxford University Press.

Jay, M. (2006). The lifeworld and lived experience. In H. Dreyfus & M. Wrathall (Eds.), *A companion to phenomenology and existentialism* (pp. 91–104). Oxford, England: Blackwell Publishing.

Luft, S. (1998). Husserl's phenomenological discovery of the natural attitude. *Continental Philosophy Review 31,* 153–170.

Mølbak, R. (2011, April 11). Lived experience as a strife between earth and world: Toward a radical phenomenological understanding of the empirical. *Journal of Theoretical and Philosophical Psychology.* Advance online publication. doi: 10.1037/a0023192

Moran, D. (2000). *Introduction to phenomenology.* New York: Routledge.

Piedmont, R. (1998). *The revised NEO personality inventory: Clinical research applications.* New York: Plenum Press.

Thombs, D. (1994). *Introduction to addictive behaviors.* New York: The Guilford Press.

9

The Role of Discipline in a Person's World

This chapter defines what a discipline is. It explores the benefits of increasing one's capacity to say "yes" and to say "no" to oneself. This capacity is crucial for the person in recovery, because it supports the development of disciplines that actually change a person's life over time.

Another term for discipline is "self-control" or, even better yet, "self-regulation." In this context, it is the ability to say "yes" to oneself (and mean it) and the concomitant ability to say "no" to oneself (and mean that too). When a person says "yes" to one thing, he or she often has also made a decision to say "no" to something else. "Shall I have eggs or cereal for breakfast? I'll have the eggs [and I won't have the cereal]." After breakfast, I contemplate what I will do that morning. I decide to go to Dockyard, and that means that I will not go to St. Georges. Why? Because Dockyard is at the west end of the island of Bermuda and St. Georges is at the other end. Although Bermuda is not all that big, and one could certainly see both in a day, it's not possible to really explore both or do anything of substance in both during one morning.

DISCIPLINE

Discipline is a form of training. A follower of Christ in the Bible, for instance, was called a disciple because he or she was a learner of the teachings of Jesus and His ways of living. A parent disciplines his or her children so that they might not grow up to be *undisciplined* (meaning unruly, chaotic, and otherwise unproductive or socially out of step). There are various things a person can do to exercise discipline, and these boil down to rewards and punishments—often the natural consequences of pursuing this or that interest. A person can give something wanted or withhold something wanted. This is behaviorism, and in one sense gestalt therapy has been called a phenomenological behaviorism (Kepner & Brien, 1970; Nevis, 2008). Certainly, any time a parent disciplines a child, that parent becomes an effective force in the child's field. Interest develops on the part of the child—perhaps only interest in what pleases the parent and prevents punishment, but the overall result is one of training, channeling, focusing, and refining. In one sense, then, learning is a matter of identifying what "works" to get or keep what one wants (where "want" can include interest as well as need).

A discipline is also a focused or dedicated field of training. In that sense, martial arts is a discipline—a broad one composed of several approaches to practicing that discipline. In such a field of training, one can be said to "practice" it, which means that people are continually "in" training and growing with respect to their expertise and competence within their discipline. Counseling is a discipline. Clinical psychology is a discipline.

There is still another sense of the word *discipline*, and that refers to the actual practices one adheres to when observing one's discipline. It is a form of self-training. As such, going through the motions of various moves in martial arts can be described as practicing the disciplines of that dedicated field of training. Meditation could be described as a discipline of certain forms of Eastern spiritual practice.

In this sense, a discipline is something a person does. In all likelihood, they do not wait until they *feel* like doing it. They just do it. They do it, because this is what they are about. This discipline in some way fits with their life. It is either a part of some surely chosen path or the initial investigations of such a path. In some way, it answers the question, "What kind of a person do I want to be right now?"

The disciplines involved in a program of recovery provide points at which one says yes or no to oneself. I will get out of the house and attend my meeting tonight. That means I will say *yes* to the meeting and *no* to staying home. Although I may want to stay home, and although the easy way might be to stay home, each time I say yes to the difficult but prorecovery discipline, I get stronger in my ability to do so. This ability to say yes and no to oneself is something that must be worked at. It is a byproduct of being diligent about the disciplines of one's recovery, and the more a person is able to say yes or no to oneself the stronger that person becomes. It is like weight training; the more you lift the stronger you get. The stronger you get, the greater your capacity to work. In recovery, the practice of well-chosen disciplines has a twofold benefit: the disciplines themselves help, and the "lifting" one does in observing them builds the capacity to say yes and no to oneself—so when that urge and temptation comes along, one is trained in the experience of saying yes and no. That is when the trained/disciplined person will say yes to recovery and no to relapse.

RELATION TO CLINICAL PRACTICE

Obviously, gestalt therapy is a discipline, and this book describes one way to practice a gestalt therapy approach to working with addictions and self-medicating behaviors. Beyond that let me suggest that there are two broad approaches a person can take in responding to psychological need. One can use medications to ameliorate symptoms, or one can deal with lifestyle in the attempt to address causal patterns. That is, admittedly, a simplistic way of putting it—but broadly, it's still true.

Think of a person who is attempting to lose weight. That person can take pills to dampen the appetite, but as soon as he or she stops taking the pills, the appetite comes back. A person can also go on a diet and lose weight. However, as soon as that person goes off the diet, the weight returns. What is needed in both cases is a lifestyle change that either supplants medication and diet or complements them. In lifestyle change, a person permanently alters the way that he or she eats and what is eaten. The weight comes off, and it stays off.

In addiction work, people can "go on a diet" by going away to a residential treatment program, but unless they change their lifestyle, they will most likely "put the weight back on" after they return to their usual environment. To change one's lifestyle, a person usually needs to practice a program, and that leads back to the concept of discipline (and practicing a discipline). The change in lifestyle is accomplished by changing behavior. Changing behavior results from purposefully practicing various disciplines across a range of domains or spheres of a person's life. These spheres contain worlds, and these worlds comprise horizons and attitudes. For instance, consider the physical domain of life (see Chapter 10). It could be seen to contain the world of physical exercise, the world of nutrition, the world of rest and relaxation, and the world of health. Overall, one could also simply refer to this as the physical world.

When disciplines are purposefully developed within these worlds, the life is enriched, the possibilities begin to expand and multiply, and the exponential effect of lifestyle change emerges in ways that cannot be determined ahead of time. One must simply be about the business of practicing various disciplines, and the change—the long-term change—emerges as paradoxical recovery.

SELF-REGULATION

This process of deciding about what disciplines to practice—or for that matter to which disciplines in life one belongs—comes under the category of self-regulation. Self-regulation is a term important to gestalt therapy, but it's a construct that certainly transcends gestalt therapy. Indeed, one way of looking at it is that self-regulation refers to the executive capacities of a person, but it was referred to in early gestalt literature as metabolism, or mental metabolism (Brownell, 2009). The former association to metabolism reflects the idea that balance and homeostasis are the dynamic principles of self-regulation. That is still somewhat true, but people see it as a bit more complex than that now.

Essentially, self-regulation is accomplished through creative adjustment to changing biopsychosocial demands. If one starts climbing a mountain in the sunshine, with a gentle breeze, one needs to change something when the breeze becomes a gale, the thunderheads roll in, hail begins to fall, and lightning threatens. One takes shelter as best one can, and the process of adjusting to the ongoing current of changing conditions in one's field is called *self-regulation* (Mann, 2010).

Expanded Definition

Self-regulation has been variously referred to and expressed for many years in gestalt therapy. In 1999, Sylvia Crocker provided an expanded definition of it by saying it addressed the question of how a person uses awareness to "solve increasingly complex problems of contact with the environmental field" (Crocker, 1999, p. 47). She identified six ways in which people self-regulate: *through interested excitement* (taking interest and mobilizing to seek solutions to emergent problems); *decision making* (identifying through thought and imagination alternative solutions, ranking them, and then identifying with one of them); *choosing* (moving to action so as to implement one's best solutions); *whole making* (making perceptual, cognitive, meaningful, and historical whole patterns that organize life); *habit formation* (learning a behavior so as to create a procedural memory); *contact and withdrawal* (being available to one's environment or withdrawing to rest, regenerate, and assimilate experience).[1]

The process of self-regulation, as can be seen, involves decision making. It requires awareness of self in a given situation, and it involves choosing among alternatives. Although the description by Crocker, stated earlier, reflects the deliberative and more cognitive approach commonly seen in research on decision making (Feldman & Beehr, 2011), there is also evidence that "going with the gut," or using an affective strategy, can be more effective in complex demands (Mikels, Maglio, Reed, & Kaplowitz, 2011). In an interesting article analyzing the decision-making strategies of Adolph Hitler as Commander in Chief, Dörner and Güss (2011) discussed various aspects of self-regulation that bridge the cognitive and affective perspectives and expand on Crocker's description. They attempted to explain Hitler's decision making by using a general theory of human action regulation called Psi, which postulates decision making as a cognitive process affected by motivation and emotion. It identifies five sets of needs. The first is existential in nature, and they are such things as hunger, avoidance of pain, and thirst. The second concerns sexuality. The third is the social need for affiliation or belonging. The fourth is the need for predictability or for the security of certainty. The fifth is the need for competence.

> *Certainty* is a psychological parameter, namely, the feeling of being able to predict future events and further developments.... *Competence* refers to one's ability to cope successfully with problems and to change aspects of the environment. (Dörner & Güss, 2011, pp. 37–38)

It makes sense that if using or drinking has become centrifugal (another way of saying the lifeworld has been shrink-wrapped around the drug of choice or self-medicating behavior), then the interest normally arising in other attitudes, corresponding to other worlds, would be unrecognized, and self-regulation as a capacity would suffer. Indeed, that is the case. In gestalt therapy terms, the addict loses the capacity to think creatively, discover or invent creative adjustments, and self-regulation takes predictable and boring pathways. When sensation arises, the addict's customary route is through drinking and drugging—through gambling, sex, eating, spending, and so on.

Self-Regulation Over Time

Over time, if one does anything frequently enough, it becomes part of the procedural memory. If that becomes petrified, some would say it leads to character distortion (Burley & Freier, 2004). That, however, is not the focus here. I am pointing to lifestyle change. Just as contact over time results in relationship, self-regulation over time results in lifestyle.

One's lifestyle is life in all its rough possibilities, chipped away by the artist's chisel and formed into a piece of craftsmanship. The self is the artist of life, working through contact and creative adjustment to self-regulate according to what is interesting and needed and perceived to be possible and available. So a person can be said to "live an interesting life." The converse, of course, can also be true.

In responding to Karl Jasper's *Psychology of Worldviews*, Martin Heidegger said, "Life is understood as experiencing, as having an experience, understanding, appropriating, and thus…as something like our *'being there' in* such experiencing" (Heidegger, 1998, p. 13). Life is being there in the thick of it and doing something with that situation.

Thus, to pick up on things said before, the addict is situated; he or she is—*there!* Recovery can be thought of as the process of "getting a life." The addict may be limited, but he or she is still in the world and among others. The raw material and the opportunities are there. What remains to be done is to engage in the discipline of self-regulation with regard to various possible worlds. Without this, there is not simply an atrophy or a withering of all possible worlds, but there is a loss of self. Creative adjustment is the essential function of the self; so, "… if once the creative functions of self-regulating, welcoming novelty, destroying and reintegrating experience—if once this work has been nullified, there is not much left to constitute a theory of the self" (Perls, Hefferline, & Goodman, 1951, p. 247). Indeed, then, the collapse of the lifeworld, and the shrink-wrapping involved, is ultimately a loss of the self—the impoverishment of life.

It is the work of the gestalt therapist to use a modified phenomenological method, a dialogical relationship, field–theoretical strategies, and all in an experimental and experiential approach that leads to paradoxical recovery. It is an approach characterized by contact that is modeled and supported. Little by little the client is encouraged through the presence of the therapist, by means of which even information is imparted, and the tracking of experience is carried out. The client becomes increasingly aware of what he or she has been doing and how he or she has been doing it. Gradually, through this therapy of contact, a restoration of the self develops. Then, the processes of decision making and self-regulation become more exciting and effective:

...contact involves not only a sense of one's self, but also the sense of whatever impinges at this boundary, whatever looms at the contact boundary and even merges into it. Skill at discriminating the universe into self and not-self transforms this paradox into an exciting, choice-making experience. (Polster & Polster, 1973, p. 103)

The structure of recovery, then, is a matter of creating disciplines that emerge from the gestalt process and inhabit diverse worlds corresponding to various domains in life. Consider Figure 9.1, which depicts various domains of life, and into each something is moving. That something is not yet clear. Perhaps it is a discipline, something the client decides to begin doing on a regular basis. Perhaps it is an emerging world in which the client will begin to experience a growing interest in a progressively, aesthetically rich attitude. The self-regulation of the client, responding to conditions in the environment through awareness work and other influences in the field will contribute to it; however, these domains form a suggested starting place.

Other people might identify different domains. If five therapists asked their respective clients to identify the domains of their lives, there might be many different configurations to consider. Use these as a suggestion and a starting place. As such, they are the physical domain, the affective domain, the cognitive domain, the relational domain, and the spiritual domain. Each of these domains, with typical disciplines that fill them up, will be developed in subsequent chapters. These are not

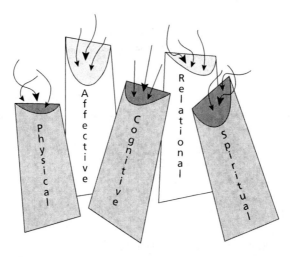

FIGURE 9.1   Dimensions and Disciplines

interventions to be prescribed like medication to achieve a particular result. It is important to remember that the gestalt approach is not like that. Rather, these are just what they sound like. They are domains of life in which a human being will likely have some interest, manifest at least one horizon, and even develop a world of related activity. These domains provide a structure for the experimental exploration of the addict's actual life, a reclaiming of the territory lost to addiction, and a scaffold next to which one can observe disciplines conducive to relapse prevention.

This growth in awareness and development of interest, including the adoption of disciplines that help give birth to worlds and enrich horizons, comprises the shaping of the addict's program of recovery. It does not necessarily supplant what was learned previously. It is not a one-size-fits-all kind of program, for as will be seen, the adoption of disciplines in these domains of life is highly individualistic, natural, and dependent on the need and interest emerging in the client's field. If someone has not been to residential treatment already, this can become one way of building a program of recovery from the ground up. If they have been to residential treatment, this can be a way of helping the client through a transition process that simply must take place if he or she is to adapt the one-size-fits-all approach learned in residential treatment and make it their own tailor-made program, unique to their respective biopsychosocial context.

GILBERT

Gil had started off on the locked unit where people detox and where low-functioning people with heavy addiction and co-occurring severe psychological disorder spend most of their time in treatment. He quickly realized he did not want to remain there; so, he went to all the groups, started meeting one-to-one with his therapist, and cooperated with the staff. After he himself had all the alcohol out of his system, he was moved over to what everyone called "the other side."

On the other side, people met in community meeting every day, and as well there were several smaller groups; some residents participated in some groups and other residents went to other groups. Everyone had his or her own therapist to learn concepts, terms, and practices, and to process what it meant to be "in recovery." The program also supported a weekly 12-step meeting.

Gil found that he could easily relate to the sense of being out of control—that the alcohol had control of him. He began to see the situation as if he had a disease called alcoholism, and he started to admit to himself that he might actually *be* an alcoholic. It sounded terrible. He felt defective and ashamed.

Gil learned the relapse cycle. He learned about "fail safe" mechanisms used to identify his triggers and establish ways to cope with them. Gil was rehearsed in numerous thinking errors used by addicts to rationalize drinking or using. He checked all these off on his personalized treatment plan, which, when he compared with other residents' personalized plans, looked very similar. Regardless, the residents chuckled about it, and they admitted they needed something, so "no bid deal."

The most helpful part of the residential program as far as Gil was concerned was the time he got to meet with his therapist. The two of them clicked with one another almost immediately, and Gil was able to talk freely. He told the therapist that when he grew up his father used to get drunk and turn into another person—a mean person who didn't like anybody and didn't like himself. It was not fun to be around him when he drank, and so people usually tried to stay out of his way during the times they learned he'd be drinking. As he grew up, he told himself he would *never* become like his father. He would never become an alcoholic. It was not an easy few sessions getting to the point at which he had to admit he'd done exactly that; it tore him up. He had gone back to his room and threw his bedding all over the place. It scared staff and residents, and that earned him a sojourn back to the locked unit. Fortunately, his doctor met with him again over there, and after a couple of days Gil was back on "the other side."

He felt himself changing. When he spoke with Michelle on the phone, he found himself using treatment language—using terms he had recently learned and using them in the idiom customary to the treatment center. It was like learning a different accent, which really amounts to another dialect.

> Michelle told him one night, "You don't sound like yourself. Are you okay?"
>
> Gil told his therapist about this, and the therapist cautioned him, saying, "It will probably be difficult when you get back. Home won't have community group in it. You won't have me to talk with, and your wife won't speak the language."
>
> Gil was concerned. "I don't know if I can make it then."
>
> "It will be important to have a follow-up plan, and someone to meet with. There are probably some 12-step groups in your area. They might be AA or NA, or even CodA."
>
> "Translation please."

"Sorry. AA is Alcoholics Anonymous, NA is Narcotics Anonymous, and CodA is Codependents Anonymous. You would do well to get your own therapist and attend AA groups every night of the week, just to be safe."

"I'm scared. You don't know what it's like in Bermuda."

"I know what it's like to come out of residential and have to make the transition. I don't care where a person is, the journey requires the same kind of thing."

"I've got a lot to lose."

"Yes. You do. You've also got a lot to gain. Don't you think? And it's worth a good try, isn't it?"

"I guess. Can I take you along in my pocket?"

The therapist smiled. He said, "Just remember what I said: 'It's worth a good try, isn't it?' "

NOTE

1. cf. Brownell, 2009, p. 67.

REFERENCES

Brownell, P. (2009). Executive functions: A neuropsychological understanding of self-regulation. *Gestalt Review, 13*(1), 62–81.

Burley, T., & Freier, C. (2004). Character structure: A gestalt-cognitive theory. *Psychotherapy: Theory, Research, Practice, and Training, 41*(3), 321–331.

Crocker, S. (1999). *A well-lived life: Essays in gestalt therapy.* Cambridge, MA: GIC Press.

Dörner, D., & Güss, C. (2011). A psychological analysis of Adolf Hitler's decision making as commander in chief: Summa Confidetia at Nimius Metus. *Review of General Psychology, 15*(1), 37–49.

Feldman, D., & Beehr, T. (2011). A three-phase model of retirement decision making. *American Psychologist, 66*(3), 193–203.

Heidegger, M. (1998). Comments on Karl Jasper's psychology of worldviews (J. van Buren, Trans.). In W. McNeill (Ed.), *Pathmarks* (pp. 1–38). Cambridge, England: Cambridge University Press.

Kepner, E., & Brien, L. (1970). Gestalt therapy and behavioristic phenomenology. In J. Fagan & I. Shepherd (Eds.), *Gestalt therapy now* (pp. 39–46). New York, NY: Science and Behavior Books.

Mann, D. (2010). *Gestalt therapy: 100 key points and techniques.* New York, NY: Routledge.

Mikels, J., Maglio, S., Reed, A., & Kaplowitz, L. (2011). Should I go with my gut? Investigating the benefits of emotion-focused decision making. *Emotion*, n.p. doi: 10.1037/a00223986

Nevis, E. (2008). Book cover comments. In P. Brownell (Ed.), *Handbook for theory, research, and practice in gestalt therapy*. Newcastle, England: Cambridge Scholars Publishing.

Perls, F., Hefferline, R., & Goodman, P. (1951). *Gestalt therapy: Excitement and growth in the human personality*. London, England: Souvenir Press.

Polster, E., & Polster, M. (1973). *Gestalt therapy integrated: Contours of theory and practice*. New York, NY: Random House.

10

Your Client's Body—The Physical Horizon

This chapter describes one's physical attitude and one's sense of embodiment and gives examples of disciplines conducive to recovery in a person's physical horizon. For example, three disciplines potential to a person's physical horizon are exercise, diet, and sleep.

THE BODY IN GESTALT THERAPY

The body has a central place in gestalt therapy, and various writers have invested a great deal of attention to it. Two come to mind: James Kepner and Ruella Frank. They each have books on the subject, with Kepner taking a more general approach and treating body process and Frank specializing in infant development and the way movement affects development from childhood through adulthood. The reader is encouraged to read what they have written[1] as it will augment what I say in this section. Beyond that, the sense of being present and engaged in any situation is linked to the bodily felt sense (Ikemi, 2005), which is also intrinsic to gestalt process: the sense of living in situations, a *Befindlichkeit* that relies on Heidegger's realization that our starting point for any experience is an embodied and situated existence. Experience is not static but constantly in motion—a constant current of process that includes the physical domain of life. Therefore, to start here with the physical domain makes sense, because it is a concrete and easily grasped domain and because it is so basic to the gestalt therapy approach.

Having said that, it may seem to the average gestalt therapist that we have deviated from mainline gestalt therapy and begun a sojourn into existential phenomenological psychotherapy, or some kind of behaviorism. The fact is that gestalt therapy is a phenomenological approach that, through its experiential/experimental dimensions, has features reminiscent of behaviorism's operant conditioning—a person follows interest, has experience, evaluates that experience, and either builds on that experience or rejects it for another kind of experience based on its value or benefit. That is creative adjustment and self-regulation. The organism assimilates what is novel and nourishing. This is gestalt therapy 101. Perls, Hefferline, and Goodman (1951) claimed that contact was foremost the awareness of assimilable novelty and behavior addressed toward it.

> Growth is the function of the contact-boundary in the organism/environment field; it is by means of creative adjustment, change, and growth that the complicated organic unities live on in the larger unity of the field. (Perls, Hefferline, & Goodman, 1951, p. 230)

In all of these domains and their respective disciplines, what I am talking about is the experimental offering of novelty. If a client is familiar with something, he or she may not be "in touch" with that knowledge, or the benefits might not be apparent, or they might have been rejected as not assimilable for them. In that case, it is fine. The idea is to expand the realm of possibilities for the client's horizon so as to increase interest, enrich the attitude, and contribute to the building of worlds that lead to a person "getting a life."

Some of these disciplines will likely prove beneficial on their own.

EXERCISE

Physical exercise is known to be beneficial in the prevention, or even treatment, of heart disease. There is also considerable research evidence that it has positive effects on the brain, emotions, one's state of mind, and one's quality of life (Atlantis, Chow, Kirby, & Singh, 2006; Fox, Hammack, & Fall, 2008; Greenwood, Strong, Dorey, & Fleshner, 2007; Lindwall, Larsman, & Haggar, 2011; Motl & McAuley, 2009; Tkachuk & Martin, 1999; Volkow, 2011; Williams et al., 2010).

Table 10.1 displays the benefits of exercise.[2]

This discipline of exercise has the potential, as will be seen in all of these disciplines, to open up a new realm of activity and interest for

TABLE 10-1
Benefits of Physical Exercise

Category	Benefit
Physical health	Cardiovascular and physical stamina
Brain function	Lowers risk of dementia and Alzheimer's disease, associated with neurogenesis, increases neuronal survival, increases blood supply to the brain
Cognitive	Improves attention, learning, and memory
Emotional	Associated with improved treatment outcomes for both depression and anxiety, effective in managing posttraumatic stress disorder, reduces stress
Quality of life	Increases a person's judgment about how well he or she is living based on physical, social, psychological, and spiritual domains; facilitates sleep

the client. It is to the addict's advantage to not only exercise but also get involved with the discipline. For the gestalt therapist, it is worth noting what the client does and how the client does it. Does he or she simply go out and run around the block in a pair of jeans, or does the person get a running outfit, get some books on the subject, get his or her own water bottle, and get special shoes? Does the client run alone or with others? Take note of how much energy and how much attention, imagination, and thought go into practicing the discipline. Does the client go to a gym and mix cardio with strength training? Does he or she get into the culture and ethos at the gym or does the client experience social awkwardness and navigate the gym as if it were a mine field?

Explore with the client in session the experience that the client has out of session. Remember that this is not about causing a predetermined effect (although exercise is proven to be helpful). At this stage of the process, it is about processing and debriefing an out-of-session experiment. There is no success or failure to it, even if the client does not do it.

If the client doesn't exercise, after having indicated he or she would, then the process becomes about how the client did not do it and what it's like to be reporting that at the current moment to the therapist. This is important because awareness of self is a great skill for an addicted person to develop. The more one learns to pay attention to what one is doing, the less likely he or she is to wander into relapse and the more purposeful that person becomes in his or her choices. This, incidentally, is mindfulness, which "... is an exemplar of the experiential mode of conscious processing and concerns a receptive state of mind wherein attention, informed by a sensitive awareness of what is occurring in the present, simply observes what is taking place ..." (Brown, Ryan, Creswell, & Niemiec, 2008, p. 75).

It is also gestalt therapy and has been so since the early middle of the last century.

If the client says he or she has done it—they have gone running or they have gone to the gym—then there is still processing to do. What was it like? What did you notice? Tell me what you were doing before you decided to run (or whatever it was). Did you schedule it or did you do it on a whim here and there? How did you accomplish this, and how will you turn it into a discipline that begins to take up residence in your life?

The idea is to conduct a gestalt analysis of the experiment to include as much of the detail of the foreground and background of the exercise as possible. Through a dialogical inquiry, the therapist explores the phenomenality of the client with respect to the exercise he or she did.

NUTRITION

In much the same way as has been explained for exercise, nutrition is another discipline possible in the physical domain. I am not a nutritionist, but this is not about going on a special diet—as if there were a gestalt diet. This is about finding out what foods are good for you and then eating them. It's also about not eating what is not good for you.

Also, the point is that this is the addict's work. The therapist does not suddenly become a health food advocate. The therapist might suggest that nutrition be explored as one discipline that the client might find interesting.

Some people get very far into this interest and create a huge world for themselves there. They not only observe eating some kinds of food and not others, but they also make this a specialty, and they advocate certain eating habits. They find out about the effects of various foods and how those foods can affect one's mental state.

Nutrition is one factor in the overall program for recovery, especially so in people suffering from alcoholism, as the alcoholic can suffer from nutritional deficits (Bradbury-Golas, 2009). People in recovery have been known to have dysfunctional eating habits that often contribute to excessive weight gain. Food is sometimes used to self-sooth in the absence of a drug of choice. A study by Cowan and Devine (2008) revealed three themes with regard to the use of food at various stages of recovery: excessive weight gain, meaningful use of food, and disordered eating with a struggle to eat healthily. People in early recovery tend to engage in mood and binge eating, using food as a substitute for the drug and to satisfy craving. People in midrecovery to late recovery complain about weight gain and typically make an effort to control their weight. Their study suggested a relationship between nutrition and general environment during recovery such that nutrition proved to be a factor in the recovering addict's field. Thus, some attention to this area might prevent a simple switch from one substance to another, say from alcohol to candy, pastries, high carbohydrates, and the kind of high caloric diet that does not help the overall picture.

SLEEP

Rest is important. Sleep is reparative. However, sleep cycles in drug addiction have a mixed array of features. Generally, drugs can be used to help a person sleep, and drugs can interfere with sleep; habitual use can interfere with sleep cycles even after detox (Asaad, Ghanem, Abdel Samee, & El-Habiby, 2011; Patrick et al., 2011; Peters, Fucito, Novosad, Toll, & O'Malley, 2011).

This category is not strictly about sleep. Sleep is the most obvious figure in speaking about rest, but here I would include the whole topic of rest and relaxation. Thus, recreation is relevant as well. People can take an interest in how to relax, in what is called "self-care." Part of good self-care is learning how to attend to one's need for sleep, need for relaxation, and need for reinvigorating oneself. This can be dedicating oneself to creating the conditions that would support sleep, taking a walk on the beach, making a date for oneself at the spa, or getting a massage. There are many relaxation techniques that a client might try out, using the various senses: auditory DVDs, visual painting and pictures, and olfactory scents that evoke a soothing response from a person's core. Finally, we come back to the issue of mindfulness, for that is a great approach to dealing with stress, and there is evidence that stress reduction/processing is the best way to treat insomnia (Brand, Gerber, Pühse, & Holsboer-Trachsler, 2010).

DISCIPLINES

Exercise
- 30 Minutes of aerobic exercise daily
- Strength training several times a week
- Flexibility/stretching

Sleep
- Get 6 to 8 hours (usually) each day
- Develop routines supportive of sleep

Nutrition
- Consult with a nutritionist
- Watch glycemic index/blood-sugar metabolism
- Create your own "recovery diet"

NOTES

1. I recommend Kepner, J. (2001). *Body process: A gestalt approach to working with the body in psychotherapy.* Cambridge, MA: GestaltPress, and Frank, R. (2001). *Body of awareness: a somatic and developmental approach to psychotherapy.* Cambridge, MA: GestaltPress.
2. Some of these studies included animal research extrapolated to human beings. It is not ethical to put a person on the treadmill and then slice up his or her brain to see what happened.

REFERENCES

Asaad, T., Ghanem, M., Abdel Samee, A., & El-Habiby, M. (2011). Sleep profile in patients with chronic opioid abuse: A polysomnographic evaluation in an Egyptian sample. *Addictive Disorders & Their Treatment, 10*(1), 21–28.

Atlantis, E., Chow, C-M., Kirby, A., & Singh, M. (2006). Worksite intervention effects on sleep quality: A randomized controlled trial. *Journal of Occupational Health Psychology, 11*(4), 291–304.

Bradbury-Golas, K. (2009). Addiction and health promotion. In A. Browne-Miller (Ed.), *The Praeger international collection on addictions, vol. 2: Psychobiological profiles, Praeger perspectives: Abnormal psychology* (pp. 3–17). Santa Barbara, CA: Praeger/ABC-CLIO.

Brand, S., Gerber, M., Pühse, U., & Holsboer-Trachsler, E. (2010). Depression, hypomania, and dysfunctional sleep-related cognitions as mediators between stress and insomnia: The best advice is not always found on the pillow! *International Journal of Stress Management, 17*(2), 114–134.

Brown, K., Ryan, R., Creswell, J., & Niemiec, C. (2008). Beyond me: Mindful responses to social threat. In H. Wayment & J. Bauer (Eds.), *Transcending self-interest: Psychological explorations of the quiet ego, decade of behavior* (pp. 75–84). Washington, DC: American Psychological Association.

Cowan, J., & Devine, C. (2008). Food, eating, and weight concerns of men in recovery from substance addiction. *Appetite, 50*(1), 33–42.

Fox, J., Hammack, S., & Fall, W. (2008). Exercise is associated with reduction in the anxiogenic effect of mCPP on acoustic startle. *Behavioral Neuroscience, 122*(4), 943–948.

Greenwood, B., Strong, P., Dorey, A., & Fleshner, M. (2007). Therapeutic effects of exercise: Wheel running reverses stress-induced interference with shuttle box escape. *Behavioral Neuroscience, 121*(5), 992–1000.

Ikemi, A. (2005). Carl Rogers and Eugene Gendlin on the bodily felt sense: What they share and where they differ. *Person-Centered and Experiential Psychotherapies, 4*(1), 31–42.

Lindwall, M., Larsman, P., & Hagger, M. (2011). The reciprocal relationship between physical activity and depression in older European adults: A prospective cross-lagged panel design using SHARE data. *Health Psychology, 30*(4), 453–462.

Motl, R., & McAuley, E. (2009). Pathway between physical activity and quality of life in adults with multiple sclerosis. *Health psychology, 28*(6), 682–689.

Patrick, M., Schulenberg, J., O'Malley, P., Maggs, J., Kloska, D., Johnston, L., & Bachman, J. (2011). Age-related changes in reasons for using alcohol and marijuana from ages 18 to 30 in a national sample. *Psychology of Addictive Behaviors, 25*(2), 330–339.

Perls, F., Hefferline, R., & Goodman, P. (1951). *Gestalt therapy: Excitement and growth in the human personality.* New York, NY: Julian Press.

Peters, E., Fucito, L., Novosad, C., Toll, B., & O'Malley, S. (2011). Effect of night smoking, sleep disturbance, and their co-occurrence on smoking outcomes. *Psychology of Addictive Behaviors, 25*(1), 312–319.

Tkachuk, G., & Martin, G. (1999). Exercise therapy for patients with psychiatric disorders: Research and clinical implications. *Professional Psychology: Research and Practice, 30*(3), 275–282.

Volkow, N. (2011). Physical activity may prevent substance abuse. *NIDA Notes, 23*(4).

Williams, D., Whitely, J., Dunsiger, S., Jennings, E., Albrecht, A., Ussher, M.,...Marcus, B. (2010). Moderate intensity exercise as an adjunct to standard smoking cessation treatment for women: A pilot study. *Psychology of Addictive Behaviors, 24*(2), 349–354.

11

Your Client's Thought Life—The Cognitive Horizon

This chapter describes one's thinking patterns and gives examples of disciplines conducive to recovery in a person's cognitive horizon. This has been the mainstay of rational recovery for years, as seen in the "thinking errors" resident in a person's relapse cycle. Here, the practices of contemplation and critical thinking are described as contributing to the world of thought, the thinking person, and the reflective attitude.

In exploring the research data correlating "cognitive" and "addiction," there were about 160 different articles in the PsycInfo database concerning the linkage in some way between cognitive process and addiction. Some explored neurotransmitters; some explored the effects of drugs on prenatal cognitive development; some explored comorbid dynamics with such disorders as schizophrenia and attention deficit hyperactivity disorder (ADHD); some investigated the effects of drugs on various parts of the brain; others explored social networking, problematic and compulsive internet use, and sexual activities; still others explored the cognitive processes that contribute to stress and relapse; and some described thinking errors at the heart of pathological gambling.

The typical treatment program will use a cognitive–behavioral approach to relapse prevention, focusing on the faulty thinking patterns that addicts use to justify using the drug of their choice or engaging in compulsive self-medicating behaviors. This, however, is not a chapter on how to assimilate cognitive–behavioral therapy into gestalt therapy. Rather, this is an exploration of one's thought life, with a view to expanding the cognitive horizon and opening up such areas as contemplation and reflection and critical and constructive thinking. The client is encouraged to become a thinker and to view daily life and recovery with a thinker's attitude.

CONTEMPLATION AND REFLECTION

Contemplation is the action of looking thoughtfully at something so as to take it in. To contemplate something is to think deeply and to reflect on it. It denotes the Hebrew concept of meditation by which a person chews on something, brings it back again, and chews on it some more, over and over again. In various places in the Psalms, two concepts—one of muttering repeatedly that which is contemplated and the other of repeatedly focusing on that which is contemplated—communicate this idea of meditation.

One way of understanding this is to realize that it is literally a chewing action that is in mind, and coming from a pastoral metaphor reminiscent of shepherding sheep. A sheep is a ruminant. A ruminant is an animal having four stomachs. When the food is first chewed, it goes to the first stomach and the liquid substance is separated from the solid substance. The solid substance is then regurgitated and chewed over and over until it is thoroughly broken down and initial stages of digestion have been accomplished.

To ruminate is to chew on something, turning it over and over and breaking it down over time. This is what is captured in the Hebrew concept of meditation, and it fits well with the early concept in gestalt therapy of dental aggression.

Dental aggression is an awkward construction. The word "aggression" has unfortunate connotations, but when understood as Perls (1947) used it, aggression means to move toward and appropriate assertively that which is nourishing, interesting, and useful. The dental aggression in Perls's mind was literally the act of biting and chewing, of aggressing, destroying, breaking down, and assimilating (Staemmler, 2010).

Thus, the illustration of ruminating is classic gestalt therapy. To think contemplatively and reflectively is to chew on whatever is perceived to be interesting, nourishing, refreshing, and of potential value, and it is to meditate by bringing it back up again and again to keep chewing on it until it is completely digested and assimilated.

This is what a thinking person does. A thinking person asks, "What does it mean?" "How do I use it?" "Where can I find it?" "How is it similar," or "How is it different?" A thinking person contemplates through the use of analogy and metaphor. A thinking person uses logic and contemplates whether or not there are any internal contradictions, circularities in reasoning, arguments that do not follow, or simple lapses.

CRITICAL AND CONSTRUCTIVE THINKING

Seymour Epstein (1993, 1998, 2008, 2010) postulated two forms of processing information, and these two forms bridge this chapter and the next. In terms of the addict, Epstein's system also relates to the relapse cycle. In this chapter, I will provide a simple version of the relapse cycle and relate that to Epstein's theory, advocating for a critical thinking approach that might be helpful to a given client. Again, not everyone is the same, and the approach is experimental. The disciplines in view, then, would be the rational approach to decision making, information processing, and problem solving.

RELAPSE CYCLE

Relapse is a normal part of recovery. Often an addict will shy away from thinking about his or her last relapse, because it seems like a failure and is loaded with shame or guilt. When that happens, an opportunity is lost. It is most helpful if a person can learn from his or her experience, and so become a thinking person who can sift through the debris of a recent relapse and conduct an autopsy on it, providing answers about how to refine one's approach to recovery. Although there are affective disciplines that can help avoid relapse (see Chapter 12), becoming more of a thinking person makes recovery more effective.

If the typical relapse cycle were a clock, then significant things happen at different *times* in the process. See Figure 11.1 for an idea of what I will explain in this section. At the top, at 12 o'clock, a person is at the top of his or her game, working a program, and doing well. Between 12 o'clock and 3 o'clock, however, life happens. The person is late to work, has a flat tire, gets chewed out by the boss, has an argument, or (because good stress is still stress) gets the opportunity to present his or her ideas to the partners, go to a party, win a race, or get a raise. What an addict knows how to do, intuitively in a preverbal and experiential way with virtually the first sensation that comes to them, is to self-medicate—make bad feelings go away or celebrate good feelings by using. However, the addict who is in recovery has a conflict between prorecovery and pro-using figures of interest, so there ensues

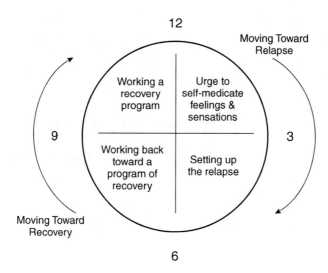

FIGURE 11.1 The Relapse Cycle

a struggle between the prorecovery mindset and the desiring-to-use mindset. That is where thinking errors emerge as rationalizations to support using. By 3 o'clock, the decision has been made in the back of the addict's head to use, but it is still not fully embraced. Between 3 o'clock and 6 o'clock, the addict sets him- or herself up to use. Circumstances are arranged to provide a compatible context and to expose oneself to influences that will make using inevitable. At 6 o'clock, the relapse occurs. Between 6 o'clock and 9 o'clock, two things take place: there is a rapid decline into intense guilt and shame, which are bad feelings that need self-medicating, so there may ensue more intense using for a period of time, and then the addict kicks out of that downward spiral (regardless of how long it takes or how short it lasts), and at 9 o'clock the addict has begun to reach out for help to start working his or her program of recovery once again. Between 9 o'clock and 12 o'clock, the addict increasingly benefits from working his or her program.

COGNITIVE–EXPERIENTIAL SELF-THEORY

Seymour Epstein (1993) described an experiential system that operates outside of awareness, is associated with emotional experience, and intuitively organizes experience while directing behavior. It operates in tandem with a rational system. Although the rational system for processing information operates by rules of inference and evidence that is linear, analytic, and abstract, the experiential system operates according to principles that are holistic, concrete, and associational. The experiential system is context specific, whereas the rational is more general. The experiential system is associated with affect and is adaptational, based on the feeling of having been in a similar situation at some other time. The experiential system gives rise to "constructive thinking," whereas the rational system gives rise to "rational (or critical) thinking."[1]

Lori Katz (2001) spoke of these two systems claiming that the rational system operates with linear, logical, analytic, and verbal modes of thinking and can rapidly adjust to changing presentations of information. It is conscious, deliberate, and intellectual, and it uses abstractions, inferences, and logic. By contrast, the experiential system is

> preconscious, automatic, associative, concrete, primarily nonverbal, affect-oriented, and holistic. It is responsive not only to direct experience but also to experience rehearsed in fantasy, vicarious experience, images, metaphors, and stories...The experiential system normally changes with repeated experience, but it can also change from an extremely emotionally charged since experience. (p. 187)

Epstein called this overall model the cognitive–experiential self-theory (CEST), and although it has some limitations with regard to gestalt therapy's model of the self, there are some ways in which it fits. The idea of a preverbal and experiential organizing influence fits with the concepts of the organism–environment and the situated agency of gestalt therapy. It is also a phenomenological approach integrating the cognitive and affective domains in an experiential motif.

Constructive Thinking

Constructive thinking is a term used to describe the automatic thoughts that emerge from the experiential system and affect both the emotional reactions and behavioral responses to stressors (Aramerman, Lynch, Donovan, Martin, & Maiso, 2001). Maladaptive constructive thinking is associated with poor adjustment to changing environmental demands; in this case, it results in intuitive and reactive responses and leaves a person vulnerable to self-medicating. Constructive thinking that is helpful uses emotions and the intuitive sense to help satisfy figures of interest, enhance creative adjustment, and facilitate effective self-regulation.

Overcoming Unproductive Constructive Thinking

Unproductive constructive thinking can be overcome through rational reprocessing, emotion-focused or experiential therapy, narrative therapy, and a number of other integrative measures (Katz, 2001). Gestalt therapy attempts to track the unaware experience to increase the client's awareness of what he or she is doing and how he or she is doing it. In terms of discipline, the client is encouraged to pay attention to his or her process and to engage in critical thinking. That discipline can be carried out through contemplation, journaling, or recording one's thoughts. The person can learn to question and challenge the ways in which intuitive actions took place and the assumptions that supported them. The goal is not to figure out "why" one is doing and what one is doing (or did what one did), but rather to notice as much as possible about how one does that thing. With hindsight, the person can ask what was going on just before one did x, y, or z? One can ask where it happened, with whom it took place, what other thoughts or feelings came up in the process, and what was accomplished by the coping strategy of constructive thinking. This is a matter of training. A person can learn the skills of critical thinking and mindfulness (for paying attention to what one is doing is being mindful) as a discipline.

In terms of relapse, a person can train him- or herself to reflect on the circumstances that resulted in a relapse. A person can think back through the steps he or she went through, moving from the desire to self-medicate bad feelings out of existence, to the rationalizations one used to justify drinking or drugging, to the ways in which one set up the relapse in question and on to the guilt or shame that propelled one into more self-medicating, and even to the ways in which he or she kicked out of the downward spiral and found a way back into recovery. All these things are worth paying attention to, but it takes discipline and a growing facility of contemplation and critical thinking to accomplish it.

DISCIPLINES

- *Journaling*: Write out thoughts, feelings, sensations, doubts—the whole of your experience as much as you can keep track of it.
- *Self-reflection and contemplation*: Focus on one aspect of your behavior or thought life and meditate on that.
- *Mindful attention to what is*: Practice this by making appointments with yourself to pay attention to what is going on around you.

- *Rational, critical analysis (postmortem) of relapse*: Slow down the "video" of your last relapse, and write out the story of it; go over this with your therapist and then take that story home and rewrite it, trying to add anything that had been left out.

NOTE

1. Epstein's theory is a highly cognitive one in nature and built on the concept of schemata. He may or may not be correct about schemata, but the emphasis is on these two approaches, generally speaking, because the distinction between them is quite useful.

REFERENCES

Aramerman, R., Lynch, K., Donovan, J., Martin, C., & Maiso, S. (2001). Constructive thinking in adolescents with substance use disorders. *Psychology of Addictive Behaviors, 15*(2), 89–96.

Epstein, S. (1993). Implications of cognitive–experiential self-theory for personality and developmental psychology. In D. Funder, R. Parke, C. Tomlinson-Keasey, & K. Widaman (Eds.), *Studying lives through time: Personality and development* (APA science volumes, pp. 399–438). Washington, DC: American Psychological Association.

Epstein, S. (1998) Cognitive-experiential self-theory: A dual-process personality theory with implications for diagnosis and psychotherapy. In R. Bornstein & J. Masling (Eds.), *Empirical perspectives on the psychoanalytic unconscious, Empirical studies of psychoanalytic theories* (Vol. 7, pp. 99–140). Washington, DC: American Psychological Association.

Epstein, S. (2008). Intuition from the perspective of cognitive–experiential self-theory. In H. Plessner, C. Tesch, & T. Betsch (Eds.), *Intuition in judgment and decision making* (pp. 23–37). Mahwah, NJ: Lawrence Erlbaum Associates Publishers.

Epstein, S. (2010). Demystifying intuition: What it is, what it does, and how it does it. *Psychological Inquiry, 21*(4), 295–312.

Katz, L. (2001). Holographic reprocessing: A cognitive–experiential psychotherapy. *Psychotherapy, 38*(2), 186–197.

Perls, F. (1947). *Ego, hunger and aggression: The gestalt therapy of sensory awakening through spontaneous personal encounter, fantasy, and contemplation.* New York: Vintage/Random House.

Staemmler, F. (June 6, 2010). *Between death instinct and education for peace: Some critical remarks on Perls's theory of aggression.* Lecture given at the conference of the Association for the Advancement of Gestalt Therapy, Philadelphia, PA, USA.

12

Your Client's Emotions—The Affective Horizon

This chapter describes one's emotional attitude and gives examples of disciplines conducive to recovery in a person's affective horizon. Emotions are the engine that drives relapse and self-medicating behaviors. The abilities to name and to be aware of one's own emotions are explored as instrumental to the capacity of processing bad feelings and self-regulating effectively.

When I worked in a dual-diagnosis (co-occurring disorders) hospital, we ran groups on relapse prevention, and we would inevitably come to the point in the process where we'd go over a number of typical thinking errors common to addiction. These are the rationalizations that make using "okay" to a person who has previously told him- or herself that he or she is in recovery and does not want to drink or drug. However, I realized that it was the experiential/emotional level of things that was the driver toward relapse, and so it always seemed to me as if the horse had already escaped the barn by the time we started talking about thinking errors. It seemed that the place to start was with the emotions, and that has been confirmed by recent study.

Both positive and negative emotions predict relapse of substance use, regardless of what substance is in question. Experiencing either positive or negative emotions has been linked to reinitiation of drug use following periods of abstinence (Witkiewitz & Wu, 2010). Other indications are that negative affect is particularly difficult. According to a model proposed by Marlatt and Witkiewitz (2005), relapse may take place when people at risk lack coping skills and are confronted with high-risk situations.

Consistent with this model, a number of studies have focused on identifying specific high-risk situations. Extensive evidence from these studies has shown that negative affect is one of the most prominent factors associated with relapse to maladaptive drinking. (Berking, Margraf, Ebert, et al., 2011, p. 307)

It would seem that emotional self-regulation is crucial to successful relapse prevention, and the areas of emotional intelligence and self-conscious emotions are, in turn, crucial in considering emotional self-regulation. To some, the highest concern is how to deal with negative emotions that pull the person in recovery down and that point to apparent faults or defects in the person him- or herself.

Disciplines that contribute to skill in emotional self-regulation provide both increased ability to say yes and no to oneself and facility in emotional regulation that supports recovery. They help open up a world of affect to a person, enriching the relational world and contributing to effective adaptation in the midst of changing environmental challenges.

EMOTIONAL INTELLIGENCE

Emotional intelligence can also be conceived of as emotional competence (EC). "Emotional competence (EC) refers to the capacity to identify, understand, express, manage, and use one's own feelings and those of others ..." (Kotsou, Nelis, Grégoire, & Mikolajczak, 2011, p. 827). Emotional intelligence/competence is one factor that enables people to adapt to social situations and work productively together. People low in this ability do not do so well and often manifest a number of interpersonal, social, and work-related difficulties or failures. Daniel Goleman (2006) characterized emotional intelligence as being composed of five features, as depicted in Table 12.1.

Emotional dysregulation is correlated to major psychological disorder, whereas high EC is related to wellness and well-being. EC is strongly correlated to mental health, physical health, and quality of relationships.

Emotional intelligence or competence can be conceived of in three ways: knowledge of one's emotions, ability to use that knowledge, and personality trait structures relevant to emotional intelligence (Nelis et al., 2011).

In terms of knowledge, if one wants to increase one's emotional intelligence, it becomes important to learn the vocabulary that corresponds with emotional experience. This is a matter of turning

TABLE 12-1
Features of Emotional Intelligence

Feature	Description
Self-awareness	Knowing what one is feeling in the moment; using affect to guide decision making
Self-regulation	Handling emotions to facilitate rather than interfere with goals
Motivation	Using our most salient interests to guide toward goals
Empathy	Sensing what other people are feeling; being able to take others' emotional perspectives
Social skills	Handling emotions in relationships and accurately reading social situations

Adapted from Goleman (2006).

the lens of awareness on oneself and then finding a term that fits. Because facial expression accounts for most of the emotional experiences (except for self-conscious emotions; see next section), a person can enlarge his or her knowledge base—the ability to recognize and name a given emotion—by finding a poster or a graphic of facial expressions, locating what one feels like at a given moment and then finding the word associated with that. This is a matter of gut feel, of correspondence. If there is a poster of facial expressions in front of a person, he or she searches the rows until suddenly *there it is!* The experience is of a match one feels in one's core instead of an idea one acknowledges in one's head.

After one knows what he or she is feeling, the next step involves what to do with that knowledge. As will be seen, there are many things that can be said about that, but what it boils down to is the ability to process emotions by expressing them into one's world in various ways.

In a study showing success in dealing with negative emotions, Kotsou et al. (2011) created a program with content and process factors that was successful for developing flexibility in dealing with difficult emotions in a relatively short period of time (with results that lasted for over a year afterward). They sought to "tame" rather than avoid or struggle with difficult emotions. Their program taught participants to observe relationships among field-relevant triggers, beliefs, thoughts, and emotions. It helped them to recognize and understand the links between emotions and thoughts and also between action tendencies and habitual behaviors. It taught people how to use various emotion-regulation strategies, for instance cultivating positive affect, as the situation might dictate, to express and listen to emotions in an adaptive way—one related to one's context and purposes—and "to use emotions and emotional situations to clarify their priorities and needs" (Kotsou et al., 2011, p. 830).

Reading the content features of that program, one can see how context sensitive that approach was. Indeed, this is the gestalt approach as well. Emotions are relative to a given situation, and the gestalt approach is a sensitive way of supporting the client in exploring what emotions he or she is experiencing and how the patterning of affective experience relates to other important interests and needs. In the Kotsou et al. (2011) study discussed previously, the process used focused on creating a context of learning to communicate emotional ability, improve self-awareness, provide experience of self, and practice experiential learning.

In terms of disciplines, then, a person can undertake to become more of an emotional person, to increase his or her emotional horizon, and to operate with an emotional attitude. This might seem counterintuitive in a world given to time management and achieving the bottom line through cognitive information-processing strategies. It might seem paradoxical to hope that learning to become more emotional might actually facilitate the processing of information, but because people are whole beings, the cognitive domain is linked to the affective domain. Focusing on emotional experience in the moment can unleash a flood of ideas and facts related to the emotion and the situation in which one experiences that emotion. Often, there is no other way to get that kind of information.

SELF-CONSCIOUS EMOTIONS

As defined by Tracy and Robins (2007), self-conscious emotions are a complex kind of emotion, which requires self-awareness and self-representation. They emerge later in childhood than do basic emotions, facilitate the attainment of complex social goals, and do not have discrete, universally recognized facial expressions.

They are distinctly a product of the situation in that the representation involved is not just the cognitive contents of the personal self but also the relational, social, and collective self-representations. "We are social creatures, so our self-representations reflect how we see ourselves vis-à-vis close others (e.g., as romantic partner), social groups (e.g., as a professor), and broader cultural collectives (e.g., as a woman, as an American)" (Tracy & Robins, 2007, p. 6).

Self-conscious emotions are evoked whenever an identity goal is in question. In gestalt therapy, this relates to personality function—the story one tells oneself about who he or she is. When the internalized public audience is perceived to observe some aspect of the person's behavior or even inner experience (such as a thought or a desire), then the person in question can experience shame, guilt, embarrassment, authentic pride, or hubristic pride.

Negative feelings about the stable and global self, "who I am," are associated with shame, whereas negative feelings about a specific behavior or action taken by the self, "what I've done," are associated with guilt.

Actions in which one feels like the public self is exposed result in embarrassment. There does not need to be any particular attribution (I did a stupid thing; I am stupid); there just needs to be an action that draws attention to the self, which suddenly feels overexposed.

Corresponding to the differences in shame and guilt, global pride is hubris in which one takes inordinate pleasure in who one is, but authentic pride is the state of being satisfied with what one has done. Hubris transcends the situation even while actually being evoked by the situation, but authentic pride is directly responsive to the specifics of a given situation and dependent on them.

Self-conscious emotions can be some of the most painful and debilitating of all emotions, and that is because they are directly linked to one's sense of self. If there were an affective correlate to the sense of smell in the physical domain, this would be it; just as the sense of smell goes directly into the brain without being mediated by any other neural system, the self-conscious emotions go directly to one's sense of self, and they affect one's experience of self without being mediated by any other system.

Shame has been written about a great deal in the gestalt literature (cf. Brownell, 2004; Lee & Wheeler, 2003; Resnick, 1997; Wheeler, 2000). In terms of addiction, the client often must deal with the sense that he or she is being judged by others and is found defective. Indeed, they have to deal with the fact that they often find themselves to be defective. This sets a person up for breaking contact, the pipeline that keeps information flowing back and forth between one person and the other. There are various ways in which a person can break contact as depicted in gestalt literature (see for instance, MacKewn, 1997, pp. 27–28; Mann, 2010, pp. 41–55; Polster & Polster, 1973, pp. 70–97).

Although one can make amends for the things he or she has done wrong, the only remedy for shame is to cease to exist. That is why the common experience of a person undergoing an episode of shame is to feel like he or she wants to run away, hide, or otherwise disappear.

DISCIPLINES

- Increase emotional vocabulary by associating emotional terms with emotional facial expressions.
- Practice feeling statements (as opposed to thinking statements).
- Try out various emotional expressions standing in front of a mirror and notice the feeling inside that is evoked with various visual countenances.
- Read books about emotional intelligence.
- Admit faults while maintaining contact in the midst of shame experiences (and so developing an increasing capacity to endure anxiety).
- Practice expressing emotions in various ways using diverse media.

REFERENCES

Berking, M., Margraf, M., Ebert, D., Wupperman, P., Hofman, S., & Junghanns, K. (2011). Deficits in emotion-regulation skills predict alcohol use during and after cognitive–behavioral therapy for alcohol dependence. *Journal of Consulting and Clinical Psychology, 79*(3), 307–318.

Brownell, P. (2004). Perceiving you perceiving me: Self-conscious emotions and gestalt therapy. *Gestalt!, 8*(1). Retrieved April 3, 2010, from http://www.g-gej.org/8-1/selfconscious.html

Goleman, D. (2006). *Working with emotional intelligence.* New York: Bantam Books.

Kotsou, I., Nelis, D., Grégoire, J., & Mikolajczak, M. (2011). Emotional plasticity: Conditions and effects of improving emotional competence in adulthood. *Journal of Applied Psychology, 96*(4), 827–839.

Lee, R., & Wheeler, G (Eds.). (2003). *The voice of shame: Silence and connection in psychotherapy.* Cambridge, MA: Gestalt Press.

MacKewn, J. (1997). *Developing gestalt counselling.* London, England: Sage.

Mann, D. (2010). *Gestalt therapy: 100 key points and techniques.* New York: Routledge.

Marlatt, G., & Witkiewitz, K. (2005). Relapse prevention for alcohol and drug problems. In G. Marlatt & D. Donovan (Eds.), *Relapse prevention: Maintenance strategies in treatment of addictive behaviors* (2nd ed., pp. 1–44). New York: The Guildford Press.

Nelis, D., Kitsou, I., Quoidbach, J., Hansenne, M., Waytens, F., Dupuis, P., & Mikolajczak, M. (2011). Increasing emotional competence improves psychological and physical well-being, social relationships, and employability. *Emotion, 11*(2), 354–366.

Polster, E., & Polster, M. (1973). *Gestalt therapy integrated: Contours of theory & practice.* New York: Vintage/Random House.

Resnick, R. (1997). The "recursive loop" of shame: An alternate gestalt therapy viewpoint. *Gestalt Review, 1*(3), 256–269.

Tracy, J., & Robins, R. (2007) The self in self-conscious emotions: A cognitive appraisal approach. In J. Tracy, R. Robins, & J. Tangney (Eds.), *The self-conscious emotions: Theory and research* (pp. 3–20). New York: The Guildford Press.

Wheeler, G. (2000). Shame and inhibition—The self in the broken field. In G. Wheeler (Ed.), *Beyond individualism: Toward a new understanding of self, relationship, and experience* (pp. 219–271). Cambridge, MA: Gestalt Press.

Witkiewitz, K., & Wu, J. (2010). Emotions and relapse in substance use: Evidence for a complex interaction among psychological, social, and biological processes. In J, Kassel (Ed.), *Substance abuse and emotion* (pp. 171–187). Washington, DC: American Psychological Association.

13

Your Client's Relationships—The Relational Horizon

This chapter describes one's relational attitude and gives examples of disciplines possible in a person's relational horizon. These include an ethical appreciation for the "other" (alterity), respect for internal and external boundaries, and maintenance of a dialogical stance (presence, acceptance, and commitment). This chapter also addresses the role of codependency and the power relationships have in self-medicating behaviors.

Relationships often play a pivotal role in a person's recovery. Frequently, a spouse or partner is driving the process into treatment, but just as often, the prorecovery efforts of a person are undermined by the significant relationship(s) in a person's life. "Couples in the initial period of recovery are often fearful, tense, silently engaged in control struggles at a covert level, and pursuing different hidden agendas. Recovery then is simultaneously a blessing and a curse" (Shields, 1989, p. 137). Often, the nature of intimate relationships in recovery must be reconsidered and renegotiated (Downs, Houghtaling, Wampler, & Shumway, 2009). Although the maintenance of friendships with people associated with the "old way of life" undermines recovery (Skinner, Haggerty, Fleming, Catalano, & Gainey, 2011), strong social ties and the building of a prosocial, prorecovery support network have proven to be protective against relapse, resulting in greater odds of recovery (Burkey, Kim, & Breakey, 2011). Just as addiction develops as a situated phenomenon, so does recovery; it involves people at various positions in a person's field (Topor, Borg, DiGirolamo, & Davidson, 2011).

BEING A RELATIONAL PERSON

Gestalt therapy started off with an emphasis on individual experience and the strategies for increasing personal awareness of contact of the individual in the environment. Many of the exercises in the first half of the Perls, Hefferline, and Goodman's (1951) text are about raising one's awareness. However, the move to contact in Polster and Polster (1973) was followed up two decades later by Hycner and Jacob (1995), and the shift to a relational perspective in gestalt therapy was well underway. It was continued in Wheeler (2000) and is explained and clarified in Yontef (2005). It's not that relationship is something new to gestalt therapy; it's just that the nascent ideas about contact evolved and expanded into the concepts more associated with relationship and found complementary interest in the wider contemporary field.

That awareness did not drop by the wayside is expressed by Hycner and Jacobs (1995) when they wrote that they hoped to show that

> a focus on dialogue does not change the Gestalt therapy emphasis on awareness as the goal of therapy *when the ontic implications of awareness are fully understood*. The awareness process which Gestalt therapy posits is a full-bodied "turning-toward" existence, that by implication is a precondition of dialogue. (p. 61)

The ontic implications indeed! To me this means that in dialogue there are really two people meeting one another—two in relationship to one another—two situated, placed as it were, and given to one another in contact over time. That means that the experience is not simply the construction of one individual; it is a coconstructed experience. The being of a person as a relational being is demonstrated through contact. Contact is a meeting with a transcendent "other"—a being similar enough to oneself to support ongoing communication and understanding, yet ontologically distinct and present. One is as situated with the other *as* the other.

Gary Yontef (2005) described this dialogical relationship as follows:

> An indispensable core aspect of the relational approach in general and the dialogic approach in particular is the commitment to dialogue, the surrender to what emerges between the participants in the dialogue when the therapist and the patient contact each other—without the therapist aiming. The paradoxical theory of change predicts that identification with ones actual state, experience, and existence is ground that supports personal growth (Beisser, 1970). When the therapist practices inclusion with authentic presence and commits to what emerges in the

contact, conditions maximum for growth and healing are created. This requires that the therapist is not committed to any predetermined outcome and can support "cultivation of uncertainty." (Yontef, 2005, n.p.)

Thus, any discipline in this area will be one that fosters an awareness of relationships. Interest in others is at the core of a relational attitude. One could nurture a healthy curiosity about others that allowed him or her to "people watch." This is not stalking. This is simply noticing and purposefully taking the time to indulge curiosity about, and interest in, others—to slow down the usual pace of life and notice what is going on around and *who* is going on around.

CONFLUENT, ENMESHED, AND CODEPENDENT

First, there is a positive sense to the concept of confluence. When rivers run together, there is a confluence (Mann, 2010), and so when lovers make love, they lose themselves in one another. However, when people lose the capacity to tolerate difference and run from difference into sameness for protection, then it is a premature confluence. Other names exist for this condition. Some people call it enmeshment, and others call it codependency. Whatever one calls it, the two have become one to avoid the contact that would reveal difference. Difference is the inevitable awareness in contact, because no two people are exactly the same. It is the fascination with, and the enjoyment of, difference that provides energy and excitement in the relationship. That is why an enmeshed relationship is also characterized by a relatively low level of energy—unless the confluence is threatened.

"A person who seeks a dysfunctional closeness in a relationship demonstrates an unwillingness to discover his or her own resources ..." (Mann, 2010, p. 54). That is what creates the sense that one person's welfare depends on what the other person does, and that is where the rub comes in terms of problematic relationships for people in recovery. It is ironic that the spouse or significant other has been wanting the addict to quit drinking or using, but when that person begins to recover, the spouse or significant other can't tolerate it. They want change, but they don't want the addicted *person* to change.

The confluent, enmeshed, and codependent significant other in a relationship with the addict will undermine the addict's recovery to keep that person from differentiating and from beginning to find his or her own resources. They need to be needed; they need to keep the addict dysfunctional and in some way dependent on them. Recovery threatens the bond and the security of the premature confluence.

The disciplines in this area of concern involve grounding oneself in one's own experience, differentiating, and establishing boundaries that support contact (or at least dissipate premature/immature confluence). Practice in mindfulness of one's current experience, to the point of being aware, literally, of one's feet on the ground, is needed to gain a sense of self, to actually have a self-experience. Following that, it is necessary to differentiate, and this requires contact and a willingness to tolerate difference. It is noticing that one's feet are here and the other's feet are there. It is noticing that one really doesn't prefer lots of butter on the popcorn (like the other usually fixes), and so on and so forth—and then it requires standing one's ground and not yielding to the pull for confluence, establishing the need for a few limits where the other's efforts (through intimidation, seduction, or manipulation) begin to seem too intrusive.

FAVORING PRORECOVERY RELATIONSHIPS

Another kind of relationship that is often problematic for someone in recovery is that between oneself and those with whom one used to drink and drug. Drug use sorts friendships (Best, Manning, & Strang, 2007; Dishion & Owen, 2009). The friends one had when *using* gave meaning to the using itself (Bell, Pavis, Cunningham-Burley, & Amos, 1998). These people will often sabotage one's recovery to "keep the party going," and they will attempt to give meaning to the addict's attempts at recovery. They, themselves, are not in recovery, and their intent is to maintain what has become for them the status quo. These people may give lip service to understanding that their friend "is trying to quit," but if their friend actually does quit, that will threaten what they used to do together. I have worked with clients whose friends actually pulled out joints in front of them to see how serious they were about quitting.

In recovery, it is often necessary to make new friends, and that can feel awkward because one's friends used to be contextualized by using. A person loses an understanding of what to do with other people, if one is not going to drink and drug. The centrifugal nature of addiction included one's friends with one's activities—getting it, preparing it, paying for it, and using it. So, if one no longer does those things anymore, what does one do with such people?

Thus, it is helpful to develop social skills conducive to making new friends, and the making of friends itself can lead to the relearning of such social skills (Glick & Rose, 2011); interpersonal experience shapes the development of social behavior. Glick and Rose (2011) discovered that high-intensity friendships are characterized by decreased blaming and increased engagement. Because addicts do a fair amount of externalizing, one discipline that might be developed would target critical and fault-finding behaviors with a view to replace them with support and acceptance of others, coupled with taking responsibility for one's own circumstances. Another discipline might target increasing involvement with, and availability to, other people; this would require that the addict develop caring for others and work on his or her ability to sustain contact.

One can establish a friend's attitude and populate a friendship horizon with relevant issues and topics and a growing list of new friends to inhabit one's social world. This process, in turn, contributes to building a new life, because new friends bring in new interests and new activities. Having a prorecovery social network has proven conducive to positive outcomes (Bohnert, German, Knowlton, & Latkin, 2010; Groh, Jason, Davis, Olson, & Ferrari, 2007).

DISCIPLINES

- Watch people (pick a public place like a bus station or a shopping mall, then sit down and watch people; develop a growing capacity to be curious about them).
- Practice contact skills such as looking, listening, touching, talking, moving, smelling, and tasting (Polster & Poster, 1973).
- Practice building others up rather than tearing others down (on the idea that to gain a friend, one must be a friend).
- Practice mindful awareness of current surroundings, one's own feelings, thoughts, values, and desires.
- Practice differentiating and boundary setting.

REFERENCES

Beisser, A. (1970). The paradoxical theory of change. In J. Fagan & I. L. Shepherd (Eds.), *Gestalt therapy now* (pp. 77–80). New York: Harper Colophon.

Bell, R., Pavis, S., Cunningham-Burley, S., & Amos. A. (1998). Young men's use of cannabis: Exploring changes in meaning and context over time. *Drugs: Education, Prevention and Policy, 5*(2), 141–155.

Best, D., Manning, V., & Strang, J. (2007). Retrospective recall of heroin initiation and the impact on peer networks. *Addiction Research & Theory, 15*(4), 397–410.

Bohnert, A., German, D., Knowlton, A., & Latkin, C. (2010). Friendship networks of inner-city adults: A latent class analysis and multi-level regression of support types and the association of supporter latent class membership with supporter and recipient drug use. *Drug and Alcohol Dependence, 107*(2–3), 134–140.

Burkey, M., Kim, Y., & Breakey, W. (2011). The role of social ties in recovery in a population of homeless substance abusers. *Addictive Disorders & Their Treatment, 10*(1), 14–20.

Dishion, T., & Owen, L. (2009). A longitudinal analysis of friendships and substance use: Bidirectional influence from adolescence to adulthood. In A. Marlatt & K. Witkiewitz (Eds.), *Addictive behaviors: New readings on etiology, prevention, and treatment* (pp. 199–224). Washington, DC: American Psychological Association.

Downs, A., Houghtaling, A., Wampler, R., & Shumway, S. (2009). Shifting perspectives in recovery: Feminist-informed relationship groups for male addicts. *Alcoholism Treatment Quarterly, 27*(4), 409–425.

Glick, G., & Rose, A. (2011). Prospective associations between friendship adjustment and social strategies: Friendship as a context for building social skills. *Developmental Psychology, 47*(4), 1117–1132.

Groh, D., Jason, L., Davis, M., Olson, B., & Ferrari, J. (2007). Friends, family, and alcohol abuse: An examination of general and alcohol-specific social support. *The American Journal of Addictions, 16*(1), 49–55.

Hycner, R., & Jacobs, L. (1995). *The healing relationship in gestalt therapy: A dialogic/self psychology approach.* Highland, NY: The Gestalt Journal Press.

Perls, F., Hefferline, R., & Goodman, P. (1951). *Gestalt therapy: Excitement and growth in the human personality.* London, England: Souvenir Press.

Polster, E., & Polster, M. (1973). *Gestalt therapy integrated: Contours of theory & practice.* New York: Vintage/Random House.

Shields, P. (1989). The recovering couples group: A viable treatment alternative. In B. Carruth & W. Mendenhall (Eds.), *Co-dependency: Issues in treatment and recovery* (pp. 135–150). London, England: Haworth Press.

Skinner, M., Haggerty, K., Fleming, C., Catalano, R., & Gainey, R. (2011). Opiate-addicted parents in methadone treatment: Long-term recovery, health, and family relationships. *Journal of Addictive Diseases, 30*(1), 17–26.

Topor, A., Borg, M., DiGirolamo, S., & Davidson L. (2011). Not just an individual journey: Social aspects of recovery. *International Journal of Social Psychiatry, 57*(1), 90–99.

Wheeler, G. (2000). *Beyond individualism: Toward a new understanding of self, relationship, & experience.* Cambridge, MA: GestaltPress.

Yontef, G. (2005). The relational attitude in gestalt theory and practice. *Gestalt!, 9*(2). Retrieved June 15, 2011, from http://www.g-gej.org/9-2/relationalgestalt.html (Republished with permission of the author and editor from the *International Gestalt Journal*, 2002, 25/1, 15–35).

14

Your Client's Ultimate Beliefs—The Spiritual Horizon

This chapter describes one's spiritual attitude and gives
examples of disciplines possible in a person's spiritual horizon.
A decidedly theistic perspective is provided here so as to
work beyond the more diffuse concept of a "higher power."
Disciplines of engagement and disengagement are offered.

RECOVERY AS A SPIRITUAL PROCESS

Spirituality and religion are important factors in recovery (Allamani, 2010; Diaz, Horton, McIlveen, Weiner, & Williams, 2011; Dodge, Krantz, & Kenny, 2010; Godlaski, 2010; Hagedorn & Moorhead, 2010; Sussman, 2010). They are major meaning-making systems in the lives of most people, and they are usually factors in the personal background and cultural context of a person (Unterrainer, Ladenhauf, Moazedi, et al., 2010).

Twelve Steps as a Spiritual System

The 12-step programs popularized by groups like AA (Alcoholics Anonymous), NA (Narcotics Anonymous), and AlAnon are spiritual systems (Hunt, 2010; Schenkeer, 2009). All one has to do is to consider the first three steps to grasp that fact. Beyond that, to work the steps will lead one into repentance, forgiveness, and reconciliation—all constructs heavily infused with a spiritual/religious tone (Table 14.1).

TABLE 14.1
Twelve Steps as a Spiritual System

Step	Declaration
1	We admitted we were powerless over our addiction—that our lives had become unmanageable
2	Came to believe that a power greater than ourselves could restore us to sanity
3	Made a decision to turn our will and our lives over to the care of God as we understood God
4	Made a searching and fearless moral inventory of ourselves
5	Admitted to God, to ourselves, and to another human being the exact nature of our wrongs
6	Were entirely ready to have God remove all these defects of character
7	Humbly asked God to remove our shortcomings
8	Made a list of all persons we had harmed and became willing to make amends to them all
9	Made direct amends to such people wherever possible, except when to do so would injure them or others
10	Continued to take personal inventory and when we were wrong promptly admitted it
11	Sought through prayer and meditation to improve our conscious contact with God as we understood God, praying only for knowledge of God's will for us and the power to carry that out
12	Having had a spiritual awakening as the result of these steps, we tried to carry this message to other addicts, and to practice these principles in all our affairs

Adapted from 12Step.org (http://www.12step.org).

WORKING WITHIN ONE'S RELIGIOUS/SPIRITUAL HOME

Not everyone will gravitate toward a Christian, or even a theistic spiritual tradition, or "home." Indeed, a gestalt therapy approach to spirituality could incorporate any number of spiritual homeworlds (Brownell, 2011a and b), and so it becomes important to address this subject from within one's own spiritual base. That can enhance the somewhat generalist approach of many 12-step groups.[1]

I will address this domain from my own frame of reference and will leave it to others to address it from theirs.

After I graduated from seminary, I joined the multiple staff of a large church in Sacramento, California. I grew up in Sacramento, so in one way it was like coming home. That church had been my home church before going away to seminary, and so, again, in another way, it was like coming home. Yet, in a more basic way, it was not getting to "home" at all.

Some say that "home" is where the heart is. As I have already said in this book, that is what some philosophers would say as well. They would say that need or interest colors one's attitude and that attitude is like a halo of interest around a person. If you are an artist then you see things in terms of colors, shapes, and composition. If you go into a large shopping mall, your artist's attitude points you in the direction of an artist's interests. You see things with the eye of an artist. Your horizon, all the things possible or that even enter the mind of an artist, allows you to think of possibilities that an artist might take advantage of in a shopping mall, and when you find a place like a crafts store, you walk in there and you feel "at home." That's because the crafts store feels like it belongs in your world. In fact, it *is* one of your worlds. That sense of home is the combination of an attitude of interest and a horizon of possibility that results in a world of being. In one's world, one says, "This is me."

I am a writer. There is a whole world of writing that opens up to me from time to time. In my world of writing are publishers, editors, and other writers. There is the excitement of potential projects, the creativity of fleshing out an initial idea, and the hard work of actually doing the writing. There is also the fascination with the finished product, because after a little while I cannot recall the drudgery part anymore, the text has grown cold, and it seems almost as if what I am reading was written by someone else. That is when I can allow myself to say, "That was pretty good!"

Into all this kind of thing—attitude, interest, need, possibility, and world—one day while working as a minister of children at this very large church, my pastor, the Senior Pastor of the church, spoke to me. I had been contemplating moving on, because as great as that very large church was, and as wonderful an experience as it had been to be on staff there (I had been ordained by that church), I had not felt that it satisfied my call to full-time Christian ministry. At that church, I had been the Minister of Children, and I loved working with the children and their families, but when I felt called to ministry, it had been to the preaching ministry—the preaching and teaching ministry. After 4 years on staff, I felt the need to find my own church. So, into that situation came this conversation between me and my pastor as I contemplated various opportunities and various places that were in need of a pastor.

My pastor told me, "A need does not constitute a call." It is remarkable to me how a person can affect you. That man was a large influence in my young life as a Christian and then also as a young minister. His words—a need does not constitute a call—have remained with me, and they seem to apply to a number of situations.

There are many, many people in need. I find them daily, if not by the hour. Of course, they come to me for help in my practice of clinical psychology, but I find them walking around the city where I live, riding the bus, visiting various locations, or eating out at various restaurants. The hospital is filled with them, and they are not always just the patients, because the staff also have needs. If a person had no way to self-regulate and was drawn to take care of every need that came his or her way, that person would become exhausted after a very short time.

I am not called to meet every need. A need does not constitute a call. Back when I was contemplating where the Lord wanted me, I was not motivated to say "yes" to every opportunity. I ultimately said "yes" to one place because, as it were, it felt like home.

Guidance from God in a manner of speaking is like discerning one's next home. God works with the natural processes of the creatures He has created, and in human beings, He works with these constructs of attitude (a sphere of interest), horizon (a sphere of possibility), and world (a sphere of being). When a person puts all these together, he or she says, "This is me. This feels like home." Put in more spiritual terminology, a person might say, "I feel called."

Called? It's the sense that God has tapped one on the shoulder and whispered, "I want you." On an experiential level, it feels right, it feels like it fits, and it's inescapable because it feels like "home." It's in keeping with one's citizenship in the Kingdom of God. In that sense, it *is* home.

It might involve going somewhere one has never been, doing something one has never done, and so it might involve the unfamiliar, but a person who is called, knows it, and the experience of the call is what makes the adventure under consideration feel like it's part of one's world.

For a need to constitute a call, it must fit with a person's homeworld. That is because guidance, which is a matter of spiritual discernment, will still involve an earthly perspective. If a human being is trying to discern the will of God, the only place that human being is going to come to know it is on earth—in his or her own world. It's where one's home is united with one's world and where a bit of heaven—the Kingdom of God—emerges on earth.

I did not come to the world of gestalt therapy as a crusade, but I do feel guided into it. It was the natural evolution of my life that moved from growing up in an alcoholic home, to becoming a neuropsychiatric technician in the Navy during the Vietnam War, to working alongside a gestalt therapist in training with Fritz Perls, to encountering Jesus and becoming a believer and follower, to becoming ordained and working in spiritual systems (called churches), to going back to school and obtaining a doctorate in clinical psychology, to getting formal training in gestalt therapy and then working with addicted and self-medicating people, people traumatized by combat and other events, and working with those struggling with spiritual/religious conflicts and issues (among other things).

Consequently, it is a calling to speak from my homeworld regarding a Christian system of spiritual discipline.

A CHRISTIAN SYSTEM OF DISCIPLINE

There are several treatments of spiritual disciplines that can inform a person at this point, and I recommend them all. In particular, I point to the following: Willard (1988), Calhoun (2005), and Foster (1998). In terms of a theistic understanding of pastoral care within a gestalt therapy framework, I recommend Norberg (2006).

Because life has a rhythm to it, a natural tidal system of flowing in and flowing out, of cycles, and of highs and lows, I am drawn to Willard's organization of several spiritual disciplines under the categories of disciplines of engagement and disciplines of what he calls abstinence (but what I think of as *dis*engagement; Table 14.2).

When I look at that list, I see practices that put me into contact with other people, and I see practices that make me withdraw from other people, but not necessarily from God. In fact, the practices of disengagement lead one to withdraw from the usual routines one might follow while carrying out everyday life in order to make room for whatever might emerge in one's potential encounter with God. Indeed, while fasting, it has struck me how little I actually do need to eat and how much more clear the voice of God seems to come to me.

The action of turning one's life over to a higher power, for it to be truly effective, depends on filling in the blank space of that construct. Is God truly capable of handling the addiction? What does God think of the addicted one? It all depends on what kind of a God one believes one's

TABLE 14-2
Disciplines of Engagement and Disengagement

Engagement	Disengagement
Study	Solitude
Worship	Silence
Celebration	Fasting
Service	Frugality
Prayer	Chastity
Fellowship	Secrecy
Confession	Sacrifice
Submission	

Adapted from Willard (1988, p. 158).

higher power to be, and that is why it becomes helpful to use the spiritual traditions at one's disposal; they provide a wealth of information about who God is and what God is like. In that respect, I recommend Feinberg (2001), Packer (1973), and Phillips (1967). The first is rather detailed theology with a philosophical appreciation, the second is a masterful description of the benefits of experiential knowledge of God, and the third is a little gem correcting many people's misperceptions of God. Of course, there are many other books a person could consult.

Let me advocate for a moment the one discipline, or capacity, that I believe to be of most importance. It is the ability to hear from God—to actually hear *God* (Willard, 1999).

When Jesus came preaching, He did not preach the gospel of forgiveness of sins; Jesus preached the gospel of the Kingdom. He sent His disciples out to preach the gospel of the Kingdom. He would frequently tell people, "The Kingdom of God has come upon you," because it had in his presence, in his actions, and in his words. The Sermon on the Mount was, and is, a Kingdom perspective. Spiritual sensitivity, sensing God, what some would call "hearing God," is a Kingdom capacity, not just a church thing. It transcends all churches, and it is the main concern when it comes to spiritual growth.

Often, people come to me in my practice of psychotherapy, and they want to talk about spiritual matters. It does not always happen, but when it does, I often find myself asking, "Can you hear God?" It is a capacity I have learned to appreciate and to nurture.

Once I found myself in a Christian friend's home, an expansive house filled with lovely things, the latest and best of technical gadgetry at that time. I realized that I was not envious; I was hurting. The situation for me at that time was difficult; it was tough, and it seemed that my friend had it so easy. I said to God, "Don't you love me? Why are things so hard for me and apparently so easy for this man?" Now, God could have said to me what Jesus told Peter on the shores of lake Galilee when Peter looked over at John and said, "What about that man?" Jesus had told Peter, "What is that to you? You follow me." Instead, God impressed me with this thought: "You are on a different path, and I have riches for you of a different kind." Understand that this was not spiritual one-upmanship, and God was not telling me that He had better things for me; the impact of God's thought goes beyond my ability to put into words, but I got the point of it. The point was that God had not forgotten about me. God had good things for me too, but our calling, our paths, and our purposes were different.

The most important discipline that an addict can develop is that which paves the way so that he or she can hear from God, but how can one sense Him?

We walk by faith and not by sight, so how can one see God at work? How can one hear God? Some hear God's voice as an impression, and it comes in the quiet and the dark of night when they cannot sleep. Some hear God in the howling of the wind. Some hear God while reading Scripture. Sometimes God is in a tragedy. The Holy Spirit is a comforter always by one's side to encourage, to convict of sin, to lead into truth, and to support and console through difficulty; in His presence, the Kingdom of God comes upon us daily.

Those who are taught by the Spirit belong to the Kingdom of God. You find them in all churches. You can even find them outside of church. You can find them in courtrooms, prisons, and homeless shelters. You can find them in governments and business organizations. You can find them in 12-step groups, and you can certainly find them in recovery.

DISCIPLINES

- Fast 2 days each week; just drink water or vegetable juice. See what happens.
- Practice talking to God; combine solitude, in which you get alone for a period of time periodically, with talking to God about the real things of life. It's not about asking God for things; it's about sharing yourself authentically with God. Keep a journal of your experience of doing this.
- Read *Mere Christianity*, by C. S. Lewis and write in the margins of the book your questions, fears, misgivings, doubts, affirmations, and realizations while doing so.
- Read the Gospel of John in a modern translation and ask God to speak to you through the pages of the book. See what happens.
- Find Willard's book or Foster's book on spiritual disciplines and start developing the practices found in them; see if your spiritual world enlarges.

NOTE

1. I say generalist because 12 steps use the terminology God as one conceives of God. That can be many things.

REFERENCES

Allamani, A. (2010). The relationship between addiction and religion and its possible implication for care. *Substance Use & Misuse, 45*(14), 2375–2377.

Brownell, P. (2011a). Spirituality in gestalt therapy. In T. Bar Yoseph Levine (Ed.), *Gestalt therapy: Advances in theory and practice* (pp. 93–104). New York: Routledge.

Brownell, P. (2011b). Intentional spirituality. In D. Bloom & P. Brownell (Eds.), *Continuity and change: Gestalt therapy now*. Newcastle, England: Cambridge Scholars Publishing.

Calhoun, A. (2005). *Spiritual disciplines handbook: Practices that transform us.* Downers Grove, IL: IVP Books.

Diaz, N., Horton, E., McIlveen, J., Weiner, M., & Williams, L. (2011). Spirituality, religiosity and depressive symptoms among individuals in substance-abuse treatment. *Journal of Religion & Spirituality in Social Work: Social Thought, 30*(1), 71–87.

Dodge, K., Krantz, B., & Kenny, P. (2010). How can we begin to measure recovery? *Substance Abuse Treatment, Prevention, and Policy, 5*, Article 31.

Feinberg, J. (2001). *No one like him.* Wheaton, IL: Crossway Books.

Foster, R. (1998). *Celebration of discipline: The path to spiritual growth.* San Francisco, CA: Harper Collins.

Godlaski, T. (2010). Dialogue on the relationship between addiction and religion and its possible implications for care. *Substance Use & Misuse, 45*(14), 2393–2395.

Hagedorn, W., & Moorhead, H. (2010). The God-shaped hole: Addictive disorders and the search for perfection. *Counseling and Values, 55*(1), 63–78.

Hunt, D. (2010). Review of a clinician's guide to twelve step recovery. *Journal of Addictive Diseases, 29*(3), 411–412.

Norberg, T. (2006). *Consenting to grace: An introduction to gestalt pastoral care.* Staten Island, NY: Penn House Press.

Packer, J. (1973). *Knowing God.* Downer's Grove, IL: IVP Books.

Phillips, J. (1967). *Your God is too small.* New York: The Macmillan Company.

Schenkeer, M. (2009). *A clinician's guide to 12-step recovery: Integrating 12-step programs into psychotherapy.* New York: W W Norton & Co.

Sussman, S. (2010). Addiction, religion, spirituality, treatment. *Substance Use & Misuse, 45*(14), 2383–2386.

Unterrainer, H.-F., Ladenhauf, K., Moazedi, M., Wallner-Liebmann, S., Fink, A. (2010). Dimensions of religious/spiritual well-being and their relation to personality and psychological well-being. *Personality and Individual Differences, 49*(3), 192–197.

Willard, D. (1988). *The spirit of the disciplines: Understanding how God changes lives.* San Francisco, CA: Harper Collins.

Willard, D. (1999). *Hearing God: Developing a conversational relationship with God.* Downer's Grove, IL: Intervarsity Press.

IV

Paradoxical Change in Recovery

15

Living in the Present

This chapter describes living in the present, while constantly adding to or refining one's way of life.

Right now, as I write this, there is a degenerating high-pressure system over Bermuda. Winds from the north had cooled the temperatures and dried out the humidity, leaving the mid-70s to mid-80s feeling very nice. However, the winds are beginning to shift around now, because a wave is forming on a stationary low front south of us. The low is growing in strength. Humidity is increasing. By this evening, there should be rain, with a chance of thunderstorms. Still, right this instant, there is a gentle breeze outside, and the clouds are providing shade for our house, the cats are napping, and I'm about ready to go fix myself some lunch.

All we have is right now. Contained in the current moment is my memory of the past and my expectation of the future, but both of those are current phenomena. That is gestalt's field perspective, but it's been part of gestalt therapy for decades (Crocker & Philippson, 2005; Truscott, 2010; Yontef, 1993; Yontef & Fuhr, 2005). In fact, it's something that has become a staple of psychotherapy in general, regardless of what perspective organizes a therapist's work (Arundale, 2011; Cepeda & Davenport, 2006; Hoffman, 2010; Farmer & Chapman, 2008; Kasper, Hill, & Kivlighan, 2008). Most approaches to psychotherapy agree that therapeutic work in the "here and now" has the greatest power to bring about change (Stern, 2004).

Any huge trip begins with one, single, first step. That step takes place in a moment of time. The next step takes place in the same moment, and that moment is identified as "now." No matter what step you take, you always take it right "now." The now is a constantly moving target that always remains steady; it's always this current moment, but it's always in the process of arriving.

Tarence Gorski (1989) identified several phases of recovery: transition (in which one gives up trying to control the drug of choice), stabilization (in which a person recuperates from the damage caused by ingesting the drug), early recovery (in which there is internal change in the way one thinks, feels, and intends to act with regard to using the drug), middle recovery (in which one repairs the lifestyle damage caused by addiction and develops a more healthy lifestyle), late recovery (in which a person grows beyond childish and developmentally stuck limitations), and maintenance (in which one experiences consistently balanced living and growth). However, it is not possible to achieve them all rapidly.

I am suggesting, with all the emphasis these days on mindfulness and acceptance, and given the well-known fact that a focus on the current moment in psychotherapy is most helpful, that perhaps the addict might make that an emphatic aspect of his or her recovery. Live in the present. Live one day at a time—it's a standard saying in self-help groups, but it's got some power to it.

Second to that, I advocate that a person live with awareness in that current moment. This kind of awareness is an embodied phenomenon. It is impossible to achieve it without paying attention to what one is sensing, perceiving, and feeling. Our bodies position us in space and in relationship to others. One's view is perspectival and limited to one's bodily position or physical place in the environment. When one contemplates what he or she is aware of at any given moment, it is an awareness fashioned from using a physical instrument. Just as a musician can practice playing an oboe or a guitar, and in the process become good at making music, a person can practice paying attention and playing his or her body, and in the process, he or she can become more and more aware.

Much of the anxiety and depression associated with substance-abuse disorders are correlated to worry about the future and regret or self-condemnation about the past. Although it is prudent to plan, and it is often necessary to make amends, one misses out on life by focusing too much on what might happen in the future and what did happen in the past. Right now is when things are currently happening, and right now is when there is the greatest opportunity to make a difference in one's life.

Once, while talking with a client and gaining some perspective on family relationships, the client was describing her mother. Her mother had died. As she spoke about her mother, her voice quality trembled, and a ripple of emotion spread across her face.

I said, "What is that?"

She stopped describing the past and said, "I miss my mother." Her words were congruent with her affect, and she looked at me with eyes that filled up with tears and a brow that sank in sadness.

I looked into her eyes. I could feel the heaviness in my chest. I let it come through my voice, and I said, "I am so sorry for your loss."

We sat for a moment in grief, smiling at one another through our tears.

That kind of bittersweet experience, shared with another person, turns suffering around. That is because negative emotion can be replaced with positive emotion, and life memories can be changed through corrective experience in the here and now.

GILBERT

The therapist said, "You've been back now two weeks. Take stock of where you're at and describe that for me."

Gil said, "I started going to meetings every day, like they told me to do." He made a face.

"What's that face mean?"

"The meeting on Tuesday night is a bust. Monday was great, and I felt right at home. The people there are serious about what they're doing. So, I went on Tuesday and there were a bunch of guys telling war stories. And one of them was drunk! I don't need that."

"You look puzzled."

"Right. I am afraid of not doing everything the treatment center told me to do."

"I am imagining there is a danger in there somewhere?"

"I'm afraid of slipping up and drinking again."

"You have to do everything just like they told you to do it? Just like as if you were still there?"

"I guess."

"I'm wondering how you do that. Where are you going to go for relapse prevention group? And where is your therapist to meet with you every day?"

"Well I meet with you, and I'm supposed to read over all my material from the center and go to AA every day."

"You can't afford to meet with me every day, and if you go to the Tuesday AA group you'll be with people who aren't serious about recovery."

"*Tell* me about it!"

"So, what are you going to do?"

"I guess I'll just have to do the best I can."

"I like that." The therapist was smiling.

"What are you smiling about?"

"You've got to make the one-size-fits-all program you learned away out there, fit your real life back here. You've got to adjust it to work for you...I notice your leg started bouncing."

Gil frowned. "I can't afford to blow it," he said. "I've started feeling discouraged, and I'm scared. Sometimes I just want to hide from everything, but if I call in sick, they'll think I'm drinking again. Melissa won't understand either."

"That feels pretty heavy."

"Try living in *my* body!"

"Speaking of your body, have you been taking care of yourself? Eating and sleeping okay? Working out?"

"Not exercising. I sleep okay. Maybe too much."

"Would you like to experiment with something?"

"What?"

"Can you run or walk strenuously for about 30 minutes a day?"

"What is that supposed to do?"

"I don't know if it will do anything. Exercise helps some people deal with stress, anxiety, and depression. Let's see what happens when you give it a good shot, shall we?"

Gil thought about it and then agreed. He decided he'd go for a run every morning before going to work.

REFERENCES

Arundale, J. (2011). Here and now interpretations. In J. Arundale & D. Bellman (Eds.), *Transference and countertransference: A unifying focus of psychoanalysis* (pp. 27–43). London, England: Karnac Books.

Cepeda, L., & Davenport, D. (2006). Person-centered therapy and solution-focused brief therapy: An integration of present and future awareness. *Psychotherapy: Theory, Research, Practice, Training, 43*(1), 1–12.

Crocker, S., & Philippson, P. (2005). Phenomenology, existentialism, and Eastern thought in gestalt therapy. In A. Woldt & S. Toman (Eds.), *Gestalt therapy history, theory, and practice* (pp. 65–80). London, England: Sage.

Farmer, R., & Chapman, A. (2008). Acceptance- and mindfulness-based interventions. In R. Farmer & A. Chapman (Eds.), *Behavioral interventions in cognitive behavior therapy: Practical guidance for putting theory into action* (pp. 251–278). Washington, DC: American Psychological Association

Gorski, T. (1989). *Passages through recovery: An action plan for preventing relapse.* Center City, MN: Hazelden.

Hoffman, L. (2010). Working with the God image in therapy: An experiential approach. *Journal of Psychology and Christianity, 29*(3), 268–271.

Kasper, L., Hill, C., & Kivlighan, D. (2008). Therapist immediacy in brief psychotherapy: Case study I. *Psychotherapy: Theory, Research, Practice, Training,* *45*(3), 281–297.

Stern, D. (2004). *The present moment in psychotherapy and everyday life.* New York: W.W. Norton & Company.

Truscott, S. (2010). Gestalt therapy. In D. Truscott (Ed.), *Becoming an effective psychotherapist: Adopting a theory of psychotherapy tha's right for you and your client* (pp. 83–96). Washington, DC: American Psychological Association.

Yontef, G. (1993). *Awareness, dialogue and process: Essays on gestalt therapy.* Highland, NY: Gestalt Journal Press.

Yontef, G., & Fuhr, R. (2005). Gestalt therapy theory of change. In A. Woldt & S. Toman (Eds.), *Gestalt therapy history, theory, and practice* (pp. 81–100). London, England: Sage.

16

Working One's Own Program

This chapter explains the process and necessity of making any program one's own program, thus of personalizing the action steps that make this program unique to oneself.

This is not an involved concept, but it is an important one. It is much easier to manage a program, which is an organized and structured set of behaviors, than it is to manage one's self. In the managing-one's-self approach, a person says things like, "I'll get to that" and "I meant to do that." The intention is a good intention, but it is seldom tied down to a point in time and space. Putting things on a calendar is a form of creating a program. A program is a schedule and an order of events. *It is a plan of action that implements a strategy.*

There are various examples of such plans of action (Hazelden, 2010; Killeen et al., 2011; Piderman, Schneekloth, Pankratz, Stevens, & Altchuler, 2008; Vakili, Currie, & el-Guebaly, 2009; Wong, Marshall, Kerr, Lai, & Wood, 2009). They exist for any organized approach to treating a population and can be thought of as logical extensions of a treatment plan.

When a person goes away to a residential treatment program, the staff there have treatment goals in mind, and they have created a program that allows them to meet the goals they set for each resident. When the residents arrive, they do not generally tell the staff what they will do (some may try, but that doesn't work). The staff has a plan, and they let each resident know what it is. The resident either buys into the program that existed before the resident arrived, or he or she does not (at which point that person usually terminates treatment early). The treatment program comes with a calendar that tells people when treatment groups meet, when they can eat, when they can sleep, when they are supposed to gather for community meeting, and when they can meet individually with their therapist. A typical program form that might be seen at a typical residential treatment center is given in Table 16.1.

The treatment program is scheduled and planned so the staff can meet their goals with reference to each resident, chart on progress, and make sure each resident meets each benchmark and checks off each tick box on the program. There is often a binder for each resident in which content materials can be stored for reading and actual check boxes can be used to mark progress. All this is highly structured, and the physical manifestations of it are external to each person, both residents and staff. People can look on the clock and know where they are supposed to be at any given time. They can look at the calendar and know how far along in the program they are. Such a structure is easier to manage than a diffuse and well-intentioned desire to remain in recovery.

The gestalt therapist working with someone in recovery can help that person by facilitating the creation of a transition structure that is also external. In the process, the gestalt therapist working with someone in recovery can suggest such structure dialogically and experimentally. The gestalt therapist can communicate research evidence that supports the development of various disciplines, and the therapist can assist the client in creating the structure needed to establish a transition program that will pick up the addict and carry him or her from residential treatment through outpatient and community-based recovery. A large part of this can be seen as working with the field and being an influence in the life space of the client. It is done experimentally and dialogically, because one never knows how a client will respond or in what direction a client might take any particular suggestion. Working sensitively with individual differences, the therapist can suggest more or less structure to this or that client.

Not every person can afford to go away to a residential treatment program, or will want to. In many cases, it becomes necessary to start from scratch with someone and, within the framework of a dialogical relationship, start building the structures of a program that fit and can be tolerated by the client. This is a slower and more tenuous process, and it is characterized by periods of discouragement, anxiety, and often relapse. It might be that for weeks that the client is not honest with the therapist and keeps using or drinking without disclosing it. Often, family members get involved and demand progress or interfere with therapy by inserting themselves as news casters letting the therapist know what is actually going on at home. It can all get quite messy.

TABLE 16.1
Residential Treatment Program

	MONDAY	TUESDAY	WEDNESDAY	THURSDAY	FRIDAY	SATURDAY	SUNDAY
7 a.m.	Wake up and morning reflections						
8 a.m.	Breakfast						
9 a.m.	Education	RP	Exercise	CM	Education	AA	PG
10 a.m.	Swimming	Bowling	RP	Step study	PG	RP	Church (optional)
11 a.m.							
Noon	Midday snack						
1 p.m.	Triggers	RP	Life skills	Goals	Reading	Outing	Visiting and free time
2 p.m.	PG	PG	PG	PG	PG		
3 p.m.							
4 p.m.	Rest and dinner	Rest and dinner	Rest and dinner	Rest and dinner	Rest and dinner	Rest and dinner	Rest and dinner
5 p.m.							
6 p.m.	Reading	Reading	Reading	Reading	Reading	Reading	Reading
7 p.m.	CE	CE	CE	CE	CE	CE	CE
8 p.m.	RP	RP	RP	RP	RP	Free time	Devotions and free time
9 p.m.	Free time, recreation, letter writing, phone calls, and one-to-one meetings with staff						
10 p.m.	Lights out						
11 p.m.							

AA, Alcoholics Anonymous meeting; CE, creative expression; CM, community meeting; PG, process group; RP, relapse prevention.

So, creating a structured program as a way of organizing and keeping track of the process is a good way for the therapist at least to keep track of progress.

In adapting the residential treatment program to an outpatient and transitional treatment program, it will be necessary to set and keep regular appointments. It will be necessary to be diligent about keeping the boundaries of such meetings and insisting on accountability. It will be necessary to evaluate where the client is in terms of awareness and motivation around abuse and/or dependence. The therapist needs to encourage the development of a prerecovery social network, and this can be where the 12-step groups come in. It will be necessary to nurture the dialogical relationship between the therapist and client so that therapist can be supportive. It is suggested that the disciplines associated with various domains of living be used to structure the client's time, energies, and activities, with a view to enlarge his or her worlds, to add interest to multiple potential attitudes, and to help the client begin to regain/rebuild his or her life. The experience of the client who is attempting to organize and rebuild his or her life can be processed using a standard gestalt therapy approach.

All these things (and more in terms of whatever structured plan and strategy both therapist and client can work out together) are paradoxical because they become part of the process, and the process is viewed as an end in itself, not as a means to determine any particular result. Yes, of course there will be results, but the program, like all of gestalt process is experimental and unpredictable.

REFERENCES

Hazelden. (2010). Healthy living options should include treatment. *Professional Update*. No. 10.

Killeen, T., Greenfield, S., Bride, B., Cohen, L., Gordon, S., & Roman, P. (2011). Assessment and treatment of co-occurring eating disorders in privately funded addiction treatment programs. *American Journal on Addiction, 20*(3), 205–211.

Piderman, K., Schneekloth, T., Pankratz, S., Stevens, S., & Altchuler, S. (2008). Spirituality during alcoholism treatment and continuous abstinence for one year. *International Journal of Psychiatry in Medicine, 38*(4), 391–406.

Vakili, S., Currie, S., & el-Guebaly, N. (2009). Evaluating the utility of drug testing in an outpatient addiction program. *Addictive Disorders & Treatment, 8*(1), 22–32.

Wong, J., Marshall, B., Kerr, T., Lai, C., & Wood E. (2009). Addiction treatment experience among a cohort of street-involved youths and young adults. *Journal of Child & Adolescent Substance Abuse, 18*(4), 398–409.

17

Trusting in the Process

This chapter explores a commitment to the process of recovery that assimilates relapse.

As mentioned already, relapse is part of the process of recovery, and part of the gestalt therapy approach to working with addiction and self-medicating behaviors. It is not a failure or a reason for finding fault, nor it is a reason to give up. Relapse is an opportunity to learn more about the unique ways in which a given person conducts his or her addiction so as to use that information to prevent future relapse. Still, the processes of recovery in a gestalt approach are not all about relapse or relapse prevention (as important as that is). Rather, the gestalt approach is concerned with reaching a quality of life that allows the spontaneous pursuit of figures of interest that lead a person naturally into novel experience that enriches and enlarges ones attitudes of interest, horizons of possibility, and worlds of existence.

Gestalt therapy is largely about process. From the beginning, it found affinity with Eastern thought. From Zen, gestalt took the idea of being completely immersed in the process going on:

> Zen teaches that all daily activities can be done with the same kind of undivided presence in the moment, where we give ourselves wholly to whatever we do, without second-guessing ourselves, without self-consciously observing how we are doing what we are doing, without being double-minded. (Crocker & Philippson, 2005, p. 75)

Eastern spirituality is largely concerned with the way in which a person lives; it is process oriented, and it is practical, being tied to the current flow of experience. The "way," or the Tao of things, promotes a process approach to understanding life.

The Tao, or the "way," refers to direction, movement, and method of thought, while living in and with nature. Spontaneity and naturalness are its chief virtues. It focuses on method and action, with attention to the current flow of experience and awareness, and it is characterized by an acceptance of what is happening and a trusting in the flow of events (Brownell, 2010).

Thus, at any given time, the unity of gestalt praxis forms a current with a pace and a rhythm of its own. Therapy is always in motion. Sometimes the process seems like it is moving slowly and other times it suddenly takes off so that people feel like something might be out of control. Indeed, the experiments in gestalt therapy have been called "safe emergencies"; yet, all of gestalt process is experimental and so ultimately uncontrolled. This does not mean that the gestalt therapist has neither any idea what he or she is doing nor any idea about where client and therapist *are* in the process; it simply means that there is no illusion about the process being determined solely by the therapist and, ultimately, totally predictable.

The process itself is action, creating experience rather than simply talking about previously enacted experience (Roubal, 2009). The phenomenal tracking of the client and the meeting between client and therapist involve risk taking at every moment. The process involves meeting and enactment, growing in awareness through contact in the moment.

All this is like jamming among musicians. When people play improvisational music, they have no script—no score of sheet music to follow. They have to listen to one another and contribute what feels right in the moment, taking each moment as it comes, playing in the current moment what fits. There are awkward moments, and there are moments of extreme excitement when it all comes together and the music is beautiful. What makes it all work is that the musicians do not stop. They know to keep playing, and they trust in the process. This is exactly what people in recovery must do, and in particular those working through the process of recovery in conjunction with a gestalt therapist.

Gestalt therapy is about the "what" and the "how" of life, and its method is suitable for a process approach to recovery that trusts in the process. That requires faith. As Gary Yontef described it:

> An indispensable core aspect of the relational approach in general and the dialogic approach in particular is the commitment to dialogue, the surrender to what emerges between the participants in the dialogue

when the therapist and the patient contact each other—without the therapist aiming. The paradoxical theory of change predicts that identification with ones actual state, experience, and existence is ground that supports personal growth (Beisser, 1970). When the therapist practices inclusion with authentic presence and commits to what emerges in the contact, conditions maximum for growth and healing are created. This requires that the therapist is not committed to any predetermined outcome and can support "cultivation of uncertainty" (Staemmler, 1997). This also requires faith in the awareness and contact process. (Yontef, 2005, n.p.)

Therefore, the process for the therapist is to focus on the here and now, attend to experience, following a modified phenomenological method that is ultimately in the service of an overall field methodology, and keep moving on through it, maintaining the dialogical relationship. Don't stop playing.

The process for the client is to respond to therapist contact, exploring novel experience through disciplines in the various domains of life, developing interest and adding possibilities to whole new worlds, and including new people and new ways of living. Don't stop playing.

REFERENCES

Beisser, A. (1970). The paradoxical theory of change. In J. Fagan & I. L. Shepherd (Eds.), *Gestalt therapy now* (pp. 77–80). New York: Harper Colophon.

Brownell, P. (2010). *Gestalt therapy: A guide to contemporary practice.* New York: Springer Publishing.

Crocker, S., & Philippson, P. (2005). Phenomenology, existentialism, and Eastern thought in gestalt therapy. In A. Woldt, & S. Toman (Eds.), *Gestalt therapy history, theory, and practice* (pp. 65–80). London, England: Sage.

Roubal, J. (2009). Experiment: A creative phenomenon of the field. *Gestalt Review, 13*(3), 263–276.

Staemmler, F.-M. (1997). Cultivated uncertainty: An attitude for gestalt therapists. *British Gestalt Journal, 6*(1), 40–48.

Yontef, G. (2005). The relational attitude in gestalt therapy theory and practice. *Gestalt!, 9*(2). Retrieved June 15, 2001, from http://www.g-gej.org/9-2/relationalgestalt.html

18

Submitting to Community

This chapter describes the healing benefits of a recovery-oriented community.

The term "submitting" might be misleading here. It is in contrast to the person who resists the whole recovery effort and rejects its relevance for his or her life. A more apt concept here might be one of a turning toward. The addict comes to the place where he or she turns toward the recovery community to find people who understand and can support their efforts.

What is the recovery community? On one level this would be the system of self-help support groups that exist in any given locality—AA (Alcoholics Anonymous), NA (Narcotics Anonymous), AlAnon, CodA (Co-Dependents Anonymous), ACOA (Adult Children of Alcoholics), and so on. However, in today's world, this would extend to the online environment and include such resources as Sober Recovery (http://www.soberrecovery.com) and 12Step.org (http://www.12step.org). It includes the outreach and community resources of various residential treatment programs. However, what I have most in mind here is the local manifestation, the people nearby with whom it might be possible to have a face-to-face connection. Any community consists of people, individuals with whom a person can connect and build relationships.

The concept of a healing community has roots in the approach of therapeutic communities, which has been a well-documented treatment modality for addiction in the United States, with renewed interest in Europe (Broekaert, 2006; Broekaert, Vandevelde, Soyez, Yates, & Slater, 2006). The therapeutic community for the treatment of addiction originated in the 1960s as a self-help alternative to the existing treatment of that time, but contemporary therapeutic communities are more sophisticated and can be short- or long-term residential treatment programs (De Leon, 2008).

Malcolm Parlett (2009) pointed out that a community, for it to be a community, needs first to have a common identification or similarity that binds its members together and a boundary around it that contains it and sets it apart from those outside it. People in recovery certainly have both. Sometimes, they wish they had neither, for the commonality is that they are recovering from a life of ruin in addiction of some kind, and the "us" and "them" characterization is often experienced as a source of shame. In actuality, people in recovery are the most courageous and authentic people one can find. When they meet in support of one another, they tell their stories with honesty and humility, and they talk about the rough spots in life in ways one will hardly ever hear or see in the mundane and superficial mainstream of society. This is one reason why it is good for therapists to learn about the relative value of the various 12-step groups that meet in their area, because not all of them are equally mature and beneficial. For therapists who desire to work with people transitioning from residential treatment for addiction, the local recovery community is a great resource.

A prorecovery community can contextualize and normalize various struggles. They incarnate and illustrate the constructs and theories associated with the various stages of recovery. They go before, and then with wisdom, they reach back to lend a hand to those still moving on up.

There is a way in which another person enriches one's life with his or her presence—simple presence. Sometimes there is fascination with how that person is, what they do, and how they do it. At other times, that other person is quite a resource and positive influence. At still other times another person can be blunt and realistic about one's failures and misgivings. All these influences, all these effects, take place in a recovery community.

It is impossible to do it alone in recovery. Such is life, really. It's impossible to live successfully all on one's own. People need one another. There is a difference between a healthy kind of need and the sticky and clinging kind of need that latches onto a person and sucks life out of him or her. Healthy need is nourishing all the way around. Contact, relationship, and belonging are good for everyone.

The recovery community is a holding environment in which the recovering addict can find support and encouragement. There is also rebuke and accountability when that is needed.

REFERENCES

Broekaert, E. (2006). Editorial: What future for the therapeutic community in the field of addiction? A view from Europe. *Addiction, 101*(12), 1677–1678.

Broekaert, E., Vandevelde, S., Soyez, V., Yates, R., & Slater, A. (2006). The third generation of therapeutic communities: The early development of the TC for addictions in Europe. *European Addiction Research, 12*(1), 1–11.

De Leon, G. (2008). Therapeutic communities. In M. Galanter & H. Kleber (Eds.), *The American Psychiatric Publishing textbook of substance abuse treatment* (4th ed., pp. 459–475). Arlington, VA: American Psychiatric Publishing, Inc.

Parlett, M. (2009). Foreword. In B. O'Neill (Ed.), *Community, psychotherapy and life focus: A gestalt anthology of the history, theory, and practice of living in community.* Wollongong East, New South Wale, Australia: Ravenwood Press.

Conclusion

LISA

"Okay. I have not been to the clubs, and I have not had a drink for a week. However, now I realize that without a drink or two, my brain is racing on the day and I can't get to sleep at night. I'm feeling tired at work. Sometimes I'm nodding off. It's terrible!"

The therapist said, "If I were you, about now I'd be wondering if it was worth quitting."

"Right," she said.

The therapist said nothing. He waited on her. He kept the eye contact. He noticed her fidgeting, but he chose to pull it back and wait on her some more.

"Well, what do I do about it? Is there some medication I can take to get to sleep?"

The therapist said, "Yes. I believe that given your tendency to use substances, however, that might not be the first place you'd want to go."

"I don't want to get addicted to drugs while I'm trying to quit drinking. So, what else would you suggest?"

The therapist said, "Are you much into exercise?"

"No. Well, yes. I get out of bed and walk to the bathroom. Then I have to walk back." She rolled her eyes.

The therapist said, "There is a fair amount of research denoting that addicted people have trouble with sleep. Also, that insomnia can be stress related. There are two approaches to dealing with the stress that you might want to try out. There is no way of knowing ahead of time how either will go with you."

"What are they?"

"One I'll tell more about next time, but the first one is exercise. I'm won-
    dering if you'd like to do an experiment."
"Oh! Another experiment. What is it this time?"
"Well, you might like it. This could become a whole new part of your
    life. Ya never know."
"Right. Me and exercise? When pigs fly?"
"You don't have to do it. In fact, if you're not into it, I'd request that you
    not even take the first step."
"No. I'll try it. I think. What do you have in mind?"
"If you belong to a gym, then spend at least 30 minutes a day on the
    treadmill at a reasonably brisk pace. If you don't, then start out some-
    where that will take up and down a couple of hillsides and take you
    about 30 minutes to complete."
"I suppose I'll have to get a pair of running shoes and a head band…
    maybe some new running shorts. It's an excuse for a new outfit! Okay.
    I'll give it a shot."
"Great. And then we'll talk about how it went the next time I see you."
"And then you'll tell me about the other way of beating insomnia?"
"We'll talk about it then."

GILBERT

Gil struggled after he returned to the island from residential treatment. At first, he attempted to attend a meeting every day, and he went
through the treatment workbooks and papers he'd been given. He
wanted a sponsor right away, but although people were supportive, no
one volunteered to be his sponsor.

The longer he was in Alcoholics Anonymous (AA), the more he struggled with the whole concept of a "higher power." He did not regard
himself to be religious. He felt coerced into being religious because of
the emphasis on a higher power, but he wanted to cooperate with the
whole program. One day he met with his therapist to finally discuss
this.

The therapist said, "You tell me that you don't believe in a higher power,
    and then you go silent and watch me?"
"Now is where you tell me I'm blowing it, right? Now is where you're
    going to tell me I am going to experience the AA equivalent of being
    damned, right?"
"That seems to be what you imagined I was going to do. Tell me, what
    would be the opposite of what you expected me to do?"

Gilbert smiled. "I love it when you do that...It would be that you would let out a scream and shout, 'Preach it, brother. Me neither!'"

The therapist said, "Why don't you do that, then?"

Gil looked a bit startled. "And I hate it when you do that!" Then he thought about it and he screamed and said in a half loud voice, "Preach it brother. Me neither."

The therapist said, "You can do better than that. Really let her lose!"

Gilbert screamed very loudly this time, and he yelled with a full throat, "PREACH IT, BROTHER! ME NEITHER!"

They both laughed.

The therapist sighed. "I think it's a matter of trust and trusting in something beyond oneself, because up to the point when someone goes for help, that person has not been able to control the addiction. Know what I mean?"

Gil knew exactly what he meant. "Trust?"

"Is there something you can trust your addiction to? Something outside yourself?"

After some thought, Gil said, "I could trust my recovery community."

"You could? I thought you were telling me nobody would be your sponsor."

"Yes, but I trust them to know the timing on that. I think it will come in its own time."

"Ah, then. I see that in fact you are already trusting them. Could they, then, be your higher power? After all, it says, 'God as you understand God to be, right?'"

MELISSA

Melissa certainly wanted Gil to stop drinking, but she did not want anything to change in their lives together. It was his problem after all. She attended AlAnon once, and she did not like it. She had one good session with the therapist in which she realized that there was some kind of enmeshment between them. However, she did not want to think about that. She wanted Gil to come back and be her old Gil, but just without the alcohol.

When Gil did get back, Melissa attempted to get him to stay at home with her instead of going to meetings. That worked for the times when the meeting in question was not a good group, but when it came time to go to the four good meetings each week, Melissa began to fight him. She began calling the other people in those groups, "losers." She criticized him for "hanging out with a bunch of losers." She accused him of meeting a woman at those groups, and she suspected him of cheating on her.

She became more seductive sexually, and she tried to get him to give up his preoccupation with recovery work. The longer it all went, the less respect he had for her, and the more constrained he felt by her. He had become determined to change his life. He was inspired by the stories those "losers" told in group, and for the first time in his life he felt like he had found some real people. He did not want to lose them.

Gilbert came to believe there was a desperate storm brewing, and he did not know if he and Melissa would be able to weather it together. She stopped going to therapy.

PARADOXICAL RECOVERY

Recovery in the gestalt approach is paradoxical because you achieve it by not trying so hard to achieve it. You hit it by not aiming directly at it. Instead, people focus on the process. The process comprises paying attention to one's experience, how meaning is being made out of experience, and increasing awareness of what one does and how one does it. The process comprises showing up to connect with trusted others, and foremost among them is a competent therapist. The therapist in turn practices presence, acceptance, and commitment to the process of meeting. The process comprises noticing causal features in the field, those elements that exert influence in the here and now; it comprises moving to action, moving out of mere talk about past experience and into the creation, and the living through of current and corrective experience.

This process is also about the slow but sure rebuilding of the lives of one's clients. In one way or another, they must find interest and explore the potential of whole new worlds of experience. I have identified several domains of living in which such worlds can be created. If the process does not include that structure, it will include another of similar nature. Life can only consist of some basic and common elements.

Personal and subjective experience, contact with others and relationship, effective influences of the biopsychosocial field, and the move to action—all that to unravel the mystery of how any one person carries out his or her addiction and comes to do the same, hated thing over and over again. It's an interesting kind of work.

Index